DORLING KINDERSLEY DK EYEWITNESS BOOKS

CRIME & DETECTION

Hungarian warrant card

British Bow Street Runner's gun

Drill used to break into safe-deposit boxes

Police uniform used in Pennsylvania

Alarm system for detecting theft from desk drawers

British peeler's truncheon

Scene-of-crime shoe covers

Magnetic fingerprint brush

Hand print

U.S. marshal's badge

DK EYEWITNESS BOOKS

CRIME & DETECTION

British policeman's
helmet badge

Written by
BRIAN LANE

Photographed by
ANDY CRAWFORD

Al Capone's cigarette case

Scene-of-
crime kit

Black Jack Ketchum's
handcuffs

Dorling Kindersley

John Dillinger's death mask

British policeman's lamp (1930s)

California police
cloth badge

German police cap

Dorling Kindersley

LONDON, NEW YORK, DELHI, JOHANNESBURG, MUNICH,
PARIS and SYDNEY

For a full catalog, visit

[DK] www.dk.com

Project editor Kitty Blount
Art editor Carlton Hibbert
Senior managing editor Gillian Denton
Senior managing art editor Julia Harris
Production Lisa Moss
Picture research Sean Hunter
DTP designer Nicky Studdart

This Eyewitness ® Book has been conceived by
Dorling Kindersley Limited and Editions Gallimard

© 1998 Dorling Kindersley Limited
This edition © 2000 Dorling Kindersley Limited
First American edition, 1998

Published in the United States by Dorling Kindersley Publishing, Inc.
95 Madison Avenue, New York, NY 10016
4 6 8 10 9 7 5

Dorling Kindersley books are available at special discounts for bulk purchases
for sales promotions or premiums. Special editions, including personalized
covers, excerpts of existing guides, and corporate imprints can be created in
large quantities for specific needs. For more information, contact Special
Markets Dept., Dorling Kindersley Publishing, Inc., 95 Madison Ave.,
New York, NY 10016; Fax: (800) 600-9098

Library of Congress Cataloging-in-Publication Data
Lane, Brian.
Crime and detection / written by Brian Lane.
p. cm. — (Eyewitness Books; v. 74) Includes index.
Summary: Explores the many different methods used to solve crimes,
covering such topics as criminals, detectives, and forensics.
1. Crime—Juvenile literature. 2. Criminal investigation—Juvenile
literature. [1. Crime. 2. Forensic sciences. 3. Criminal investigation.]
I. Title.
HV6251.L35   2000   364—dc21   97–32376
ISBN 0-7894-8643-1

Color reproduction by Colourscan, Singapore
Printed in China by Toppan Printing Co. (Shenzhen) Ltd.

Policeman's rattle

Policewoman's
truncheon

Truncheon

British peeler's top hat

Bonnie Parker's body armor

British peeler's uniform

Contents

Prison uniform of the
type worn at Alcatraz

Crime and society

THERE ARE FEW CORNERS of the world that are free from crime. Crime is defined in the dictionary as "an act punishable by law," so its nature depends on the laws of each society. The laws of a Judeo-Christian society follow the teachings of the Bible; many of the moral values of these societies are derived from the Ten Commandments. An Islamic society adopts the wisdom of the Koran. Among many African and Asian groups, tribal rules of conduct are often decided by a council of elders, who decide both what is a crime and how to punish it. Whatever the basis of their legal system, all societies must deal with people who defy the law.

CAIN AND ABEL
According to the biblical book of Genesis, Cain, the elder son of Adam and Eve, was a farmer. He made a sacrifice of corn to God. His younger brother, Abel, a shepherd, offered his best sheep. God accepted the sheep, but rejected the corn. Moved by jealousy and anger, Cain killed his brother. This, says the Bible, was the first murder.

LOOTING AND BLACK MARKET SALES
Sometimes the results of war are destruction and lawlessness. In this confusion, some people steal goods from damaged houses and shops. This practice is called looting. The term comes from the Hindi word *lut*, which means "booty." Looting also occurs during peacetime – when there are inner-city riots, for example. Closely associated with looting is the secret selling of food and other items that are either scarce or heavily rationed. This is known as selling on the "black market."

EMPEROR JUSTINIAN
Flavius Anicius Sabbaticus Justinianus, called Justinian the Great (483–565), was a Byzantine emperor who laid the foundations of Roman law. Many of the modern world's legal systems are based on this body of law, called the Justinian Code.

DRACONIAN LAWS
Above is an extract in the original Greek of Draco's *Laws on Murder*. Draco was a lawmaker in Athens, Greece (624–621 B.C.). He ordered execution for all crimes, including laziness. He believed even minor crimes warranted death, and therefore could not find a greater punishment for more serious crimes. The term "Draconian laws" evolved from Draco's harshness.

The Artful Dodger picks a pocket while Oliver looks on in horror in a scene from Charles Dickens's novel Oliver Twist

19TH-CENTURY CRIME WAVE
The increasing wealth of factory owners brought about by the Industrial Revolution in Europe widened the gap between rich and poor, and crime grew. This illustration from *Oliver Twist* by Charles Dickens shows some pickpockets in operation. This increase in crime helped lead to the founding of police forces and the strengthening of laws and punishments. In the first quarter of the 19th century, there were 156 crimes punishable by death, including heretical preaching and monopolizing corn.

STORMING THE BASTILLE

The main prison in Paris during the French Revolution was the Bastille. In July 1789, it was stormed by a Parisian crowd and the prisoners were released. The most unusual of these liberated "prisoners" were several hundred books that had been imprisoned for the crime of being critical of the monarchy.

Contemporary print of the blazing Bastille

LAW IN VARIOUS CULTURES

Not all legal systems are based on Roman law. In parts of Africa and Asia, tribal chiefs advised by holy men administer justice. In North Africa, shamans and witch doctors dictate the law.

Lion mask of a shaman belonging to Africa's Ashanti tribe

At the time the Lindow Man was put into the bog, he wore only a strip of fox fur tied around the top of his right arm

A length of twisted root fiber was found tightened around the neck

This chest wound could have been caused by stabbing

The Lindow Man was kept in excellent condition by the preservative qualities of peat

THE CASE OF PETE MARSH

In 1984, a prehistoric corpse was unearthed from a peat bog on Lindow Moss, Cheshire, England. A medical examination revealed that the "bog man," who became known as Pete Marsh after the place he was found, had suffered many deliberate injuries – a stab wound to the chest, bludgeoning of the head, strangulation, and a cut throat – any of which could have caused his death. There can be no doubt that he was killed; the question is, was it murder, or ritual sacrifice?

Law and order

SINCE ALL SOCIETIES SUFFER CRIMES, they have all developed systems of law by which to judge wrongdoers and assist the law enforcement officers in bringing criminals to justice (pp. 12–13). Officers try to keep order by preventing people from committing crimes and thereby breaking the law. In many countries, laws fall into two categories: "common" and statutary. "Common" law is based on previous legal judgments and is often unwritten law. Statutory law is a collection of written laws, or statutes, enacted by parliaments, congresses, and legislatures.

Collar prevents garroting, or strangling from behind

Belt to which truncheon and lantern are attached

Lantern with thick, round glass front, like a bull's-eye

WOODEN RATTLE
A wooden rattle was used to signal an alarm or call for help. Rattles were carried in a pocket of one of the tails of the jacket. Rattles, rather than whistles, were used initially because hotel doormen used whistles to call cabs. By 1880, however, increasing traffic noise made whistles essential.

Double-barreled pistol of 1763 carried by a Bow Street Runner

Armband worn to show officer is on duty

Bobbys's truncheon, sometimes called a "nut-cracker"

BOW STREET RUNNERS
In 1750, crime had become such a problem in London that Sir Henry Fielding, the magistrate at Bow Street Court, assembled a force of six men to patrol the streets in and around the city. They were called Bow Street Runners because night and day they were available, within 15 minutes, to "run" after a criminal. Despite growing in numbers and effectiveness, the Runners were disbanded in 1829.

White, lightweight trousers worn in summer

Bobby's hanger (saber) and sheath worn on the belt only on ceremonial occasions

BOBBY'S UNIFORM
Sir Robert Peel was the British home secretary from 1822 to 1830. He founded the Metropolitan Police at Scotland Yard. These officers became known as "peelers" or "bobbies," shortenings of Sir Robert's name. The force was known for its distinguished uniform.

Stovepipe hat, strong enough to protect the head and sturdy enough to stand on and see over a wall

THE FIRST FRENCH POLICE
The Marquis de Louvois (left) and Gabriel La Reynie founded the police force in Paris, France, in 1667. As chief of police, La Reynie abolished the *cour des miracles*. A *cour des miracles* was an area of sanctuary in the center of each French city in which beggars and bandits hid from the law. He also introduced a mounted and a pedestrian police force in Paris.

THIEF AND DETECTIVE
When the infamous French thief François-Eugène Vidocq was released from his last term in prison in 1809, he offered to act as a spy for the French police. He recruited other ex-convicts, who used their knowledge of criminal activity to make a very effective detective force.

THE STRONG ARM OF THE LAW
Tom Smith was a familiar figure in London's West End in the 1850s. He was 6 feet 5 in (1 m 96 cm) tall and weighed over 287 lbs (130 kg). It was said he could stop a fight merely by appearing at the scene.

Stovepipe hat

Tunic collar with officer's identification number

This staff is tipped with a metal crown

SIGN OF OFFICE
Tipstaffs were used for identification. They were carried by English sheriffs' officers or bailiffs when delivering legal warrants. The officers themselves also became known as "tipstaffs."

Sheriff badge

Pinkerton detective badge

Federal marshal badge

BADGES OF OFFICE
Public officials have always needed identification to prove their authority. It is especially important for a law enforcement officer – whether a sheriff in the Wild West or a detective constable in London – to show that he or she has the power to search and arrest.

Embossed jacket buttons

Pinkerton in disguise captures a thief aboard a train

ALLAN PINKERTON
Born in Scotland in 1819, Allan Pinkerton arrived in the United States in the early 1840s. In 1850, he founded Pinkerton's National Detective Agency in Chicago. The agency still exists today. Among other feats, Pinkerton foiled an assassination attempt on Abraham Lincoln.

Frank James's revolver

Tassel from the furnishings at Jesse's funeral

WANTED: JESSE JAMES – DEAD OR ALIVE
Offer of a money reward for the capture of criminals is one method used by law enforcement agencies in an effort to maintain order. Between 1866 and 1892, Jesse James and his brother Frank headed a band of outlaws in the Wild West who robbed banks, trains, and stagecoaches, and killed at least 10 people. A $10,000 reward was offered for Jesse's capture, dead or alive.

Bullets dug out of a tree near Jesse James's hideout

A piece of Jesse James's coffin. In 1882, Jesse was shot by Bob Ford, a fellow outlaw, for a share in the reward

Long trousers were worn all year round, whatever the weather

Justice and sentencing

PILLORY
Putting minor criminals on display for the scorn and amusement of the public was first done by the ancient Greeks and Romans. In medieval times, a pillory was used. It trapped the neck and wrists of the felon. He or she was then displayed in the village square or carried through the town. The public threw rotten vegetables at the criminal; an especially disliked criminal would be pelted with stones.

IN MOST PARTS of the modern world the ideas of *justice* and *sentencing* go hand in hand. *Justice* is simply a means by which punishment can be given fairly according to the crime and the circumstances of the convicted criminal. The *sentence* is the punishment imposed. Most national laws consider crimes of violence against people very serious, and the punishments for these offenses are most severe. In a criminal action, a governmental unit asks the court to try an alleged offender. In the United States, that unit may be the local, state, or federal jurisdiction. For example, murder and robbery are generally state crimes.

CHINESE COURT
A prisoner is being brought before a magistrate in a 16th-century Chinese court. By then, China already had a very efficient legal system based on the laws of Confucius, a famous Chinese philosopher of the first century B.C.

Stroud's chess set and board, drawn inside the cover of his book Avian Anatomy

LYNCHING
Lynching is the illegal killing (usually by hanging) of an accused prisoner by a mob. The lynchers usually think that the suspected offender will escape just punishment. Lynching can include beating, burning, stoning, or hanging.

PASSING THE TIME
During his 54-year stay in prison for murder, Robert Stroud studied the diseases of canaries. He became a leading authority and wrote several books on the subject, including this one. He came to be known as "the Birdman of Alcatraz."

An English barrister, a lawyer who pleads cases in the higher courts

"THE HANGING JUDGE"
The state of Arkansas had become so lawless that in 1875 President Ulysses Grant appointed Isaac Charles Parker as a federal judge in Fort Smith. During his legal career in Jesse James territory, Parker had developed a deep hatred for lawbreakers. In 21 years on the bench, Parker issued more than 160 death sentences, earning him the name "The Hanging Judge."

DEFENSE AND PROSECUTION
In many countries, an accused person is given the chance to have his defense presented to the court by a lawyer. A prosecuting counsel presents the opposite case, maintaining the accused's guilt. A jury, a group of independent, randomly selected people, decides whether or not the prosecution has proven the accused's guilt.

COURTROOM CAPERS
This scene depicts an English police court in the early 19th century. It is possible that the violent young men facing the magistrate were arrested for being drunk and disorderly. Such scenes are extremely rare in today's courts, partly because of the fear of harsher sentences, and partly because of the presence of trained security staff.

Handcuffs used to restrain Ketchum

"BLACK JACK" KETCHUM
Ketchum was born in New Mexico in 1866. He formed a gang that specialized in train robberies, but they had little success. "Black Jack" was a heavy drinker, not afraid to use his gun. He was finally arrested after being injured in a shoot-out. He was convicted of the murder of Sheriff Edward Farr and hanged.

GUARD DUTY
Either because of the fierce guards or the ferocious currents surrounding the island, only three inmates ever managed to escape the federal prison at Alcatraz, and they have never been seen or heard of since.

Alcatraz guard's belt buckle

Prisoner's number

Prisoner's shirt of the type worn in Alcatraz

11364

GUSICK

"THE ROCK"
Alcatraz, the world's most notorious prison, was built on a rocky island in San Francisco Bay. Originally a military prison, "The Rock" served as a federal penitentiary from 1934 to 1963. Dangerous currents around the island made escape impossible. Famous inmates included Al Capone, "Machine Gun" Kelly, and Robert Stroud, "the Birdman of Alcatraz."

Bounty hunters and thief takers

Whether bounty hunters in the American Wild West or thief takers in 18th-century Britain, some people have always been ready to catch criminals for a rich reward. There were few sheriffs in the new, 19th-century towns of the United States, so bounty hunters flourished as rough-and-ready peacekeepers. Thief taking became popular in England after the passage of the Highwayman Act in 1692. This act offered large rewards for the capture of highwaymen and other criminals. If the thief takers were criminals themselves, they would be granted a pardon for bringing in the accused. This meant that it was easy for a guilty person to send an innocent one to the gallows.

A pouch of gold and silver coins, the thief taker's "blood money"

An idealized painting of Pat Garrett

THE PAYOFF
Bounty hunters and thief takers were paid well. In Britain, a thief taker earned 40 pounds, and the highwayman's horse and goods, for each convicted thief. In the United States, the bounty hunter's reward depended on the notoriety of the criminal. The first reward offered for the outlaw Jesse James was $500; the last was $25,000.

BOTH SIDES OF THE LAW
Jonathan Wild was one of London's most ruthless and powerful criminals. He also brought criminals to justice. Calling himself the "Thief Taker General of Great Britain and Ireland," he used a vast network of criminal informers to become the most famous thief taker London had ever known. He even sent some of his fellow criminals to the gallows. Wild was hanged in 1725, at the age of 43.

BILLY THE KID
Billy the Kid never went to school. Born in New York City in 1859, he was brought up on the legend of Jesse James (p. 11). He became a gambler, a rustler (a cattle and horse thief), and a killer. Billy's real name is believed to be William H. Bonney.

TRACKER
In 1880, Patrick Floyd Garrett, the sheriff of Lincoln County, New Mexico, captured the notorious outlaw Billy the Kid. The Kid escaped from jail but not from Garrett, who tracked him for three months and finally shot him dead at Fort Sumner, New Mexico, in July 1881.

DICK TURPIN
An infamous highwayman, Dick Turpin (1705–1739) robbed coaches on the busy roads near London. He tried to prevent his friend and fellow highwayman Tom King from being captured. In doing so, Turpin accidentally shot King, who later died.

Bulletproof vest worn by many bounty hunters

An employee of a bail bondsman

IN CUSTODY
Bounty hunting can still be lucrative. In the United States, if a person is arrested and offered bail, he can borrow the money, called a bail bond, from a bail bondsman for a fee. If the accused does not appear in court, the bondsman loses his money. This is when the bondsman puts bounty hunters on the fugitive's trail to recoup his money.

Reeder Webb's ivory-handled Colt gun

MODERN BOUNTY HUNTERS
In this photograph, a modern-day bounty hunter catches a criminal in Miami. More than 100 years have passed since the legendary days of the Wild West. Although the preservation of law and order is now firmly in the hands of the FBI and local police forces, independent operators still work for reward money.

SHERIFF REEDER WEBB
In 1927, the Texas Bankers' Association published an announcement: "Reward $5,000 for dead bank robbers, not one cent for live ones." According to local legend, Reeder Webb, the sheriff of Odessa, West Texas, then lured two local thieves to a bank, where he shot them and collected the reward. To this day, a picture of Webb hangs in the sheriff's office in Odessa.

Webb's leather-covered blackjack

THE MAN WITH NO NAME
This still is from the 1964 western film *A Fistful of Dollars* in which Clint Eastwood played an honorable bounty hunter. In actuality, bounty hunters in the Wild West were often no more than hired killers, who would murder anyone for a "fistful of dollars."

Sheriff Webb's brass knuckles

Theft and burglary

THEFT AND BURGLARY are classified as crimes against property. Theft covers everything from stealing an apple from a fruit stand to lifting a gold watch from a jeweler's counter. A theft is considered to be far more serious if it involves physical violence, as in the case of mugging. Burglary is entering a building for the purpose of stealing. It is considered a very serious crime, especially if the act is aggravated, for example, by the use of a gun.

Suitcases can be used to carry stolen goods from the property

MAKING A BREAK FOR IT
In 1950, a reformed burglar walked into the office of the English magazine *Picture Post* and offered to demonstrate his skills for an article on the methods used by a burglar. He staged a job and it was photographed. The former burglar stated that the general public, by failing to properly secure their homes, made burglary easy to commit.

COLONEL BLOOD
In England in 1671, Irish adventurer Thomas Blood and two accomplices, disguised as clergymen, were allowed to see the crown jewels in the Tower of London. They attempted to steal them but found most of them too bulky and heavy. Blood managed to escape with the crown, crushed and hidden under his coat. The thieves were captured when Blood's horse fell. King Charles II, impressed by the daring of the plot, gave Blood a royal pardon.

NED KELLY
Born in Australia in 1855, the son of a transported convict, Ned became a bushranger, a robber who lived in the bush, or outback. As the result of a scuffle with a policeman, he and his gang were hunted down by troopers. Only one of the soldiers survived the gun battle. For the next two years, Ned Kelly made a profitable living robbing banks. He is known for a remarkable suit of armor made from iron. He met his death on the gallows in 1880.

Wanted notices

PUBLIC ENEMY NO. 1
In 1933, at the age of 31, John Dillinger had already spent nine years in prison for theft. On his release, he formed a gang and became a notorious bank robber. Soon Dillinger was at the top of the FBI's Public Enemy list, and huge rewards were being offered for his capture, dead or alive. Finally he was betrayed by Anna Sager, an acquaintance, who became known as "the woman in red." The FBI shot Dillinger as he walked out of a movie theater in Chicago in July 1934.

GREAT TRAIN ROBBERY

In the early hours of August 8, 1963, a gang of 12 robbers stole 2.5 million pounds from the Royal Mail train traveling between London, England, and Glasgow, Scotland. They hid out at a remote farmhouse before separating with their shares of the loot. Three of the gang got away. The rest, including the three pictured here, spent lengthy terms in prison.

Train coach

Charlie Wilson   Jimmy White   Bruce Reynolds

Dillinger's wooden "gun" blackened with shoe polish

Headline announcing Dillinger's death

DILLINGER'S ESCAPE

In January 1934, Dillinger was arrested in Tucson, Arizona, and sent to Indiana to face charges of killing a poilceman. Always a clever crook, Dillinger escaped from the jail in Crown Point by waving a "gun." In fact his weapon was simply a piece of wood carved into the shape of a gun. It could not have maimed anyone.

The forks can be levered up to here to allow the ram raiders to enter at a higher level

RAM RAIDING

A new threat hit the commercial and business world in the 1990s in the form of ram raiding. Vehicles fitted with fenders made from reinforced steel girders are rammed into doors and windows of shops and warehouses, breaking open an entry for robbers. The industrial vehicle shown above is perfect for the crime because of the forks at the front.

Drill could not pierce safe

SAFE DEPOSIT BOX OPENER

In 1987, 60 million pounds were stolen from the Kensington Safe Depository Center in London. The robbers took this electric drill to the scene to get into the safes. The drill snapped and was abandoned in favor of sledgehammers. Valerio Viccei, the leader of the robbers, was caught and sentenced to 22 years in prison.

Dillinger's death mask. A mold of his face was made after his death for identification

Swindles and frauds

THE WORLD IS A LARGE MARKETPLACE, with people selling goods and services and other people buying them. But this atmosphere of commerce has a dark side to it. Wherever there is a chance to make "easy" money by dishonest means, there are untrustworthy individuals ready to take that chance. And for every criminal, there is a person willing to believe that he or she can get something cheap. A swindle or a fraud involves deliberately cheating someone out of money. They range from cardsharps fixing games at fairs so there is no chance of winning, to con artists who have managed to "sell" public monuments for huge amounts of money.

CHARLIE PEACE
A burglar and murderer of the 19th century, Charlie Peace moved in respectable and wealthy circles. He was able to live this double life because he was a brilliant master of disguise. Even his own family could not recognize him in disguise.

THE ULTIMATE BUG KILLER
Many swindlers do their business through newspaper advertisements. One ad published in a U.S. newspaper promised "a method 100% effective against cockroaches." People who sent money received two blocks of wood with the instructions: "Place cockroach on block A. Take block B and strike down hard on block A." Although it worked, the defrauder was still sent to prison.

Block B, which is brought down on the execution block to kill the cockroach

FIXING SPORTS EVENTS
There are many ways to fix sports events, from paying a boxer to take a fall, or a football player to throw a game, to drugging horses to win or lose. Swindlers try to fix sports events because they can make huge amounts of money betting (or by taking bets from others) if they know in advance who is going to win. Most sports are regulated to try to prevent this sort of manipulation from taking place.

AT SEA
False claims on insurance policies have always been a common fraud, usually in the area of merchant shipping. For example, a vessel carrying a shipment of wool would be reported wrecked and the cargo lost. Meanwhile, the ship would dock at another port. The wool would be sold and the ship would be given a new name. The owner of the wool would have the money from its sale and the insurance money for its loss. The ship-owner would still have the ship and the insurance for its loss.

Because of the sophisticated tracking equipment onboard modern cargo ships like this one, it is almost impossible to "lose" a vessel

The queen of hearts is turned facedown and shuffled among the other cards

FIND THE LADY

"Find the lady" is a trick played at fairs or on the streets with three cards, one of which is the queen of hearts. The dealer lays the cards facedown on a table, first revealing which one is the queen. He then shuffles the cards on the table and invites the audience to "find the lady." The dealer's accomplice, pretending to be an ordinary onlooker, puts money on a card repeatedly, and wins. Then others try. But without having been briefed by the dealer, they cannot find the queen.

George C. Parker sold the Statue of Liberty

CHARLES PONZI

One of the world's most successful con men, Italian-born Charles Ponzi made a fortune in the United States in 1919–20. He persuaded people to invest money in his Financial Exchange Company with the promise of high interest. In fact, the company was not making any money. The interest it paid out was the money provided by new investors.

Ponzi was convicted of fraud and served nine years in prison

CREDIT CARD FRAUD

The most common form of credit card fraud is the use of stolen cards by thieves, but some schemes are more complex. For example, in the late 1960s, Alphonse Confessore, a maintenance engineer for Diners Club who used to make fraudulent charge cards for his friends, was blackmailed into printing 1,500 fraudulent Diners Club cards for an organized crime gang. Confessore was caught and convicted, then murdered as he left court.

Cockroach on its execution block

VICTORY BONDS

Horatio Bottomley from England was a swindler, publisher, and politician. A self-styled "friend of the poor," he began the Victory Bond Club in Britain in 1919 to let poor people buy a share in the government's postwar investment. In fact, Bottomley was not investing the money, just keeping it for himself. He made £150,000 ($240,000), was accused of fraud, convicted, and sentenced to seven years in prison.

SELLING MONUMENTS

Many of the world's largest and most famous monuments have been "sold" to the gullible by charming tricksters. Probably the greatest "monumental" con man was George C. Parker, who, over 45 years, sold the Brooklyn Bridge, Madison Square Garden, President Grant's tomb, and the Statue of Liberty.

Forgery

FORGER AT WORK
Decoration is added to a fake Oriental vase. Chinese porcelain has always been a popular subject for forgers. Even modern artists' ceramic work is often copied.

THE WORDS *forgery* and *counterfeit* are usually associated with paper money. However, anything that is rare or valuable is likely to be counterfeited, and can include items ranging from ancient Egyptian relics to modern "designer" perfumes. Forgery is usually attempted for profit, prestige, or political reasons. In the time of the Pharaohs, a group of Egyptians created a counterfeit Shabaka Stone, a relic thought to prove that the world was created in their capital city of Memphis. Some counterfeiters, such as those who forge works of art, do so solely to deceive experts. The advance of scientific techniques and instruments have made forgery more detectable than ever before, decreasing a counterfeiter's chance of success.

Gold-covered bronze

GUILTY GOLDEN EAGLES
This pair of fake eagle brooches were made in the 19th century, sometimes known as the great age of faking. The eagle design was popular in the culture of the Visigoths, a Germanic people of the second through eighth centuries A.D. The originals were 4.72 in (12 cm) high and made of solid gold inlaid with precious gems. Several eagle brooches were analyzed and found to be cast bronze covered with gold sheet and inlaid with colored stones. In 1941, Amable Pozo, a Spanish jeweler, was revealed as the faker.

A fake medieval medallion

Original shabti would have carried hoes; forger mistakenly gave copy flail scepters

CASTING A FORTUNE
Shabti were small figurines that were buried with the dead of ancient Egypt. They were to act as servants and carry out any tasks required of the deceased in the afterlife. Although some fakes have been cast from original shabti, many fakes have been made from scratch. They are easy to detect with their clumsy detail and incorrect hieroglyphic inscriptions.

PLATED FORGERIES

These fake ancient "gold" coins, claimed to be from the time of Alexander the Great, were cast in copper and plated in gold. The fraud was exposed only when the plating split to reveal the bright green color of oxidized copper.

Oxidized copper

Fake shabti

Shabti mold

43407

BILLY'S AND CHARLEY'S
In the mid-19th century, Billy Smith and Charley Eaton sold genuine antiquities dug from the Thames foreshore. Demand was so great that they decided to make a few "antiquities" of their own, mostly "medieval" medallions cast in lead. Even after they were revealed as forgers, Billy and Charley continued in business until Charley's death.

THOMAS CHATTERTON
Chatterton, born in 1752, began writing his own poetry while still at school in England. In 1768, he wrote a fake medieval text that was good enough to fool local experts. At the age of 18, he traveled to London and continued to write fake medieval poems and letters. When some of his work was revealed as fake, Chatterton lost both fame and fortune. He took his own life with arsenic in 1770.

COMMERCIAL FORGERY

There was a time when perfume was just perfume. One brand cost about the same as the next to produce. Now certain designer brands have become very desirable and, as a result, cost more than other fragrances. Poor-quality copies of expensive scents are made illegally and are popular.

Out of the bottle, one perfume looks just like another

A forged 1835 Bank of Rome note

COPYCAT CURRENCY

Forging currency can be very profitable. The forger can spend the counterfeit money or sell it to other criminals. The many precautions taken today, including paper quality, watermarks, numbering, elaborate engraving and printing processes, and security devices, make it more difficult to produce a forgery that can escape detection. But in earlier times, vast sums of forged currency circulated without detection.

A genuine 1835 Bank of Rome note

FERNAND LEGROS

Legros is an eccentric French art dealer, recognizable by his signature wide-brimmed hat, beard, and dark glasses. In 1967, he was accused of having sold fake masterpieces to a now-deceased Texas multimillionaire. The canvases were painted by Hungarian forger Elmyr de Hory, who later committed suicide.

A fake Swedish 10-daler note, drawn by hand

Hitler's handwriting

Hitler's genuine 1925 appointments diary

Julius Grant with one of the fake Hitler diaries

Comparison microscope

HITLER'S DIARIES

In 1983, the West German magazine *Stern* announced the discovery of the personal diaries of Adolf Hitler. Many experts lined up to authenticate them. Vast sums of money began to change hands for publication rights. Then Julius Grant, the foremost forensic document examiner of the century, inspected the documents. Grant soon determined that the paper on which the diaries were written contained optical dyes, which were not used in the manufacture of paper until after Hitler's death. Thus the diaries proved to be fakes.

Murder and kidnapping

PEOPLE HAVE BEEN harming and killing each other for property, power, or pleasure since the dawn of time. Other people have been trying to solve these crimes and capture the people responsible for them. As new technology has been developed, so the means of detecting crimes have improved. It is becoming more and more difficult to commit a murder or kidnapping without being caught, especially with advances in forensics (pp. 44–45), but it is often a criminal's own carelessness that leads to his or her apprehension.

"ET TU, BRUTE?"
On March 15, 44 B.C., the Roman emperor Gaius Julius Caesar was stabbed to death in the Senate house by Marcus Brutus and other conspirators because they wanted to seize power. In one of the first triumphs of forensic medicine, Caesar's doctor Antistus was able to state that only one of the 23 stab wounds – the one through the emperor's heart – was fatal.

A page from Le Petit Journal *shows Detective Inspector Walter Dew arresting Crippen and his mistress, who is disguised as a boy*

ARRESTATION DU DOCTEUR CRIPPEN ET D... LE NE... SUR LE PONT DU "MONTRO...

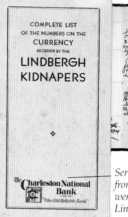

LINDBERGH ABDUCTION
In March 1932, a notorious baby kidnapping occurred. The baby's father, Charles Lindbergh, was the most famous aviator of his time. A ransom was paid, but on May 12, the infant's dead body was found. He had been killed soon after the abduction.

Serial numbers from bank notes were recorded before Lindbergh handed over the ransom money

One of the investigators Colonel Norman Schwarzkopf (father of General Schwarzkopf of Gulf War fame), recorded details of the Lindbergh case in a diary

CAPTURE OF HAWLEY HARVEY CRIPPEN
After poisoning his wife in 1910, Crippen left London with his mistress, Ethel le Neve, on a ship bound for Canada. Despite the pair's disguises, the captain was suspicious and used the newly invented telegraph system to send a telegram to Scotland Yard. A detective overtook the fugitives on a faster ship and arrested them. Crippen was tried and hanged.

Crippen's pocket watch

HAUPTMANN'S CAPTORS
In September 1934, FBI agents (above) learnt that some of Lindbergh's $50,000 ransom money had been used at a New York gas station. The attendant had taken down the license plate number. This led to the arrest of a German-born carpenter named Bruno Hauptmann, who was later tried, found guilty of the child's murder, and executed in 1936.

THE FRENCH "BLUEBEARD"
Henri-Desiré Landru used "lonely hearts" advertisements in French newspapers to meet wealthy women. He then took all their money and property and disappeared. Those women who thwarted his plans were killed. Landru murdered at least 10 women between 1915 and 1919.

Landru and Madame Segret, his mistress at the time he was arrested, who was believed to be his next intended victim

Landru at his trial at the Seine-et-Oise Assize Court in November 1921, before he was convicted and sent to the guillotine in 1922

SADAMICHI HIRASAWA
On January 26, 1948, Sadamichi Hirasawa murdered 12 employees of a Tokyo, Japan, bank. He posed as a Health Department official and told the manager that, because of a dysentery outbreak, all employees must be given a dose of medicine. Within seconds of drinking the cyanide liquid, the bank staff died. Hirasawa fled with 180,000 yen.

Hirasawa, imprisoned for murder

LEOPOLD AND LOEB
In 1924, Nathan Leopold and Richard Loeb, two American teenagers, tried to commit the perfect murder. On May 21, they stabbed 14-year-old Bobby Franks to death and sent his father a ransom note demanding $10,000. Leopold's eyeglasses were dropped near the body. This and other evidence led to the pair's conviction. They were sentenced to life imprisonment for murder and 99 years for kidnapping.

Lord Lucan's House of Lords cloak label

THE EARL OF LUCAN

Lucan's trunk, in which he carried his silver to an auction shortly before he disappeared

THE R HON THE EARL OF LUCAN No. 3.

WHERE IS "LUCKY" LUCAN?
Richard John Bingham, Seventh Earl of Lucan, known as "Lucky" to his friends, disappeared on November 7, 1974. In the home of his former wife, he left the body of Sandra Rivett, his children's nanny. In June 1975, the coroner's jury announced a verdict of "murder by Lord Lucan." Although there have been reports from all over the world that Lord Lucan has been seen alive, the sightings have never been confirmed. His fate remains a mystery!

Prohibition

On October 28, 1919, the U.S. Congress passed the National Prohibition Act, commonly known as the Volstead Act, which made the sale of alcoholic liquor illegal. At first it was a popular act, but soon it was evident that Prohibition was both absurd and unworkable. People who rarely drank became desperate to do so; people who drank a lot demanded more. This demand was being met by organized gangs who had discovered that huge amounts of money could be made. Ships carried cases of spirits to the United States from all over the world. A $15 case of smuggled whisky would be sold for $80. Rivalry between gangs was fierce and often erupted into violence in the streets.

AL "SCARFACE" CAPONE
Alphonse Capone, most notorious of the Chicago gangsters, began his career in crime in New York. In 1919, he took control of illegal alcohol distribution in Chicago. It is claimed that Capone, with 300 gunmen, was responsible for 1,000 killings.

Al Capone's silver cigarette case

Crowd looting a store of confiscated liquor

HIDING THE LIQUOR
Soon the gangs found they could make more cash by manufacturing and selling their own alcohol (bootlegging), and there was less risk involved. However, many people tired of the excessive profits made by the gangsters and decided they too could make their own, known as "bathtub gin." It was not until 1933 that Prohibition was repealed.

A sawed-off double-barreled shotgun hidden in a violin case

THE UNTOUCHABLES
Eliot Ness, born in 1902, became well known during the late 1920s as a special agent in the Prohibition Bureau of the U.S. Department of Justice. He led a team of officers, called "The Untouchables" because they could not be bribed or intimidated by gangsters, to break up the trade in illegal alcohol.

HOOVER
John Edgar Hoover rose through the ranks of the U.S. Department of Justice to become the first director of the Federal Bureau of Investigation (FBI) in 1924. During the 1930s, he attacked the problem of gangsterism and started a list of "Public Enemies." Hoover headed the FBI for 48 years, under eight presidents.

SAM GIANCANA
When Al Capone died, other mobsters, including Sam "Momo" Giancana, took over the Chicago underworld. Giancana later became the city's crime boss. He moved into gambling clubs and ended up with a large share of the Riviera Casino.

Giancana after his 1957 arrest in Chicago in connection with the murder of banker Leon Marcus

Giancana's lucky four-leaf clover

Giancana's lighters

GIANCANA'S JEWELRY
Giancana's jewelry was confiscated and returned by the law when he was arrested many times. Before the age of 20, he had been arrested three times for murder. When he took command of the Chicago Mafia, he had been arrested 60 times for charges including battery, bombing, and assault to kill. He was described as the most ruthless mobster in the United States. He was murdered in his home in 1975.

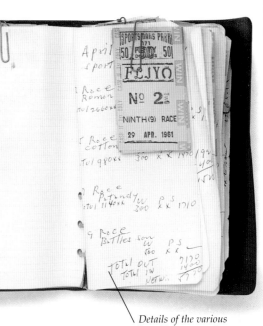

Giancana's betting book, containing winning slips only, was used as evidence of a legitimate income

CONCEALED THREATS
For obvious reasons, gangsters preferred to conceal their weapons when traveling to a "job." The most popular hiding place for shotguns and the Thompson submachine gun, or tommy gun, was a violin case. It proved surprisingly successful despite the fact that a group of "Big Al's" hoodlums were not likely to pass as the string section of the Chicago Philharmonic!

Details of the various bets Giancana made

Frank Costello, born Francesco Castiglia in Lauropolin, Italy, became known as the "prime minister" of the mob

FRANK COSTELLO
Frank Costello rose through the gangster world to control much of the country's gambling. In 1951, he was a star witness at the Kefauver Investigation. Despite the extent of his gangland crime, Costello, like Capone, was finally jailed for tax evasion.

KEFAUVER HEARINGS
The televised hearings were opened in May 1950 by Tennessee's Senator Estes Kefauver. The five-man committee spent almost two years traveling the United States interviewing hundreds of underworld figures to determine whether there was any evidence that an organized crime syndicate was in operation. Their conclusion was that such a network did exist.

International gangsters

THE MAFIA IS PROBABLY THE BEST-KNOWN organized crime gang in the world, but it is not the only one. Wherever dishonest money can be made from drugs, gambling, and moneylending, gangsters organize themselves into powerful groups to lay claim to it. Like the mobsters of Prohibition times, modern gangsters defend their territory jealously, and often violently, and new territories are constantly established. For example, the Triads, which originated in China, now have units all around the world. However, there have been great changes in the way that these modern criminals operate. Gangsters often look more like bank managers than hoodlums, and many have come to realize that there is a considerable advantage in running a respectable business to act as a cover for their dishonest deals.

MAFIA NUN
Sister Alvina Murelli, a 51-year-old nun, was arrested in 1983, in Naples, Italy, when police began a crackdown on the underworld of organized crime gangs. In the photo above, she holds a copy of the New Testament's four Gospels. She used this book to smuggle out coded messages from the mafiosi whom she visited in jail.

MONEY LAUNDERING
The main source of wealth for most gangs is the illegal trade in drugs. Drug barons usually launder their "dirty" money by filtering the cash through large "respectable" companies and banks owned or run by the gangs.

Paddle for turning cards

GAMBLING
Like the drug trade, illegal gambling is a popular source of gangland money. It provides very big returns for very little outlay, and the chances of winning are stacked against the player even if the game has not been fixed. Chinese games of chance figure very strongly in the Triad economy, and illegal basement gambling dens can be found in Chinatown districts around the world.

Card dispenser ensures that dealer's hands barely touch cards

Betting counters, called chips

Gambling cards

YAKUZA FUNERAL
The Yakuza controls most of the gangland activity in Japan. Although the members claim to have a Robin Hood image – robbing the rich to give to the poor – the Yakuza was officially outlawed in 1992 for its activities in the areas of extortion, money laundering, and gunrunning. In 1984, Masahisa Takenaka, leader of the Yamaguchi-gumi (largest of the Yakuza gangs), was killed by rivals. His funeral (left) was attended by members of the group – and 400 riot police.

Masahisa Takenaka

Giovanni Brusca was arrested at a seaside resort in Sicily

Doorway and steps carved out of stone

CAPTURING GANGSTERS

Enhanced communications systems around the globe have increased the efficiency and success rate of most of the world's police forces. In 1996, the arrest of Sicilian bomber Giovanni Brusca ended one of Italy's most intensive manhunts and marked a significant victory against the growing threat of organized crime in Sicily and Italy.

Roulette wheels are often rigged so the operator can control where the ball drops

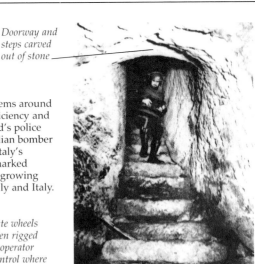

SECRET HIDEAWAYS

Communication among Mafia bosses has also improved over the years, and many meetings are held to arrange "business" deals. In 1985, Italian police broke into caves under the country villa of Michele Greco, a top Mafia leader in Sicily. Mafia leaders held summit meetings in this underground hideaway.

"RUSSIAN MAFIA"

In the confusion and disarray following the breakup of the former Soviet Union, organized crime moved in. Known as the "Russian mafia," the gangs have become ruthless, violent and increasingly bold. This violence has been met with equal brutality by the police – resulting in many funerals, such as that of mobster Vladislav Listiev (above).

ALL ON THE SPIN OF A WHEEL

One of the most popular gambling games in the big casinos is roulette. For decades, organized crime has made easy money at the roulette wheel, where corrupt casino owners run rigged games. Most of the profitable betting games, however, are card games, such as blackjack, poker, and faro.

Gamblers bet on where the ball will stop

Gambling chip

Chip sweep to gather in chips

Smuggling and piracy

SMUGGLING IS THE ILLEGAL MOVEMENT of goods in and out of countries. It is an extremely profitable crime because the smuggler avoids paying customs duties on these items. Customs duties are taxes on certain goods, such as tobacco or alcohol, that are imported into the country. There is also a profit to be made when smuggling items or substances that are banned, such as illegal drugs like cocaine and marijuana, from one country to another. Piracy, or robbery at sea, has occurred since ancient times, and involves the capture of wealth or vessels on the open seas.

OLDEST TRICK IN THE BOOK
An old method of smuggling small amounts of illegal goods is to hide them inside a hollowed-out section of a book. Another method is replacing a legal substance, such as talcum powder, with a similar-looking illegal drug.

Mandolin made from illegally exported turtle shell

ON THE EDGE OF EXTINCTION
As a result of the continuing threat to endangered wildlife, international agreements have been signed to outlaw the killing of certain birds and animals. Also banned are the export of some live creatures and the trade in animal parts, such as skins, ivory, and bones. The exquisite shell of the hawksbill turtle (left) is sold illegally as a curiosity or for making into souvenirs such as jewelry boxes.

CUSTOMS OFFICERS
Port police officers, such as these French officers in 1905 (above), are called customs officers and work to prevent smuggling. Alcohol and tobacco used to be commonly smuggled substances. Now drugs are a customs officer's main concerns.

FACE THE WALL
It was customary for villagers of the south coast of England during the 18th century to turn their faces to the wall when smugglers carried contraband from their boats. This way, the locals could not identify the smugglers when questioned by customs officers. Identification would both anger the smugglers and deprive the locals of the smuggled goods.

Shell of hawksbill turtle

SKIN OF THE JAGUAR
The jaguar is killed illegally for its coat. This skin was seized by authorities in Brazil. In many parts of the world, trade in illegal animal products provides an income that is vital for human survival. Where conservation is most needed, poverty is often greatest.

BAG CHECKING
While armed officers secure the safety of a seaport or airport, customs officers inspect passengers' baggage for smuggled goods. They usually do not check every suitcase or bag, but rely on experience, instinct, or tips (advance information) to pick out bags likely to contain smuggled goods.

X-RAY VISION
In an attempt to reduce international terrorism and smuggling, officers use equipment that can scan human beings and their luggage for concealed objects, such as guns. This device has detected bags of cocaine, knives (plastic and metal), coins, and guns.

ALWAYS ON ALERT
Smuggling is only one of the crimes that air transport police must try to prevent. Others include terrorism and large-scale theft from the airport's secure warehouses. Airports are policed by armed security officers.

Space in a pair of boots to hide drugs

HIDING THE GOODS
Getting contraband (smuggled goods) past the watchful eyes of customs officers is the smuggler's most difficult task. Countless objects have been used to conceal forbidden contraband – from hollowed-out books and statues to shoes and spare tires.

A hollowed-out sculpture

Hollow heel in a shoe

Drum ready to be filled with drugs

PIRATES
A gang of Chinese pirates (above) climb aboard to attack a ship. Pirates were not the romantic characters portrayed in literature and films. They were murderous robbers who often fought among themselves and stole from each other.

Fire!

MOST FIRES START ACCIDENTALLY – a cigarette is left burning, or a stove is left on. Arson fires, however, are started deliberately. Whatever the cause of the fire, the procedure to put it out is the same. Most countries have emergency fire departments. When the firefighters arrive at the scene, they must make sure that any occupants are taken to safety, put out the fire, and ensure that the building is safe from collapse. If there has been any loss of life, or if the fire seems to have been started deliberately, a fire investigation unit moves in. If arson is suspected because, for example, traces of gasoline have been found, the fire investigation unit works closely with the regular police force to solve the crime.

FIGHTING THE FIRE
Firefighters belong to one of the most dangerous of the emergency services. At each major incident there are three major hazards – fire and explosion, smoke inhalation, and falling debris. The firefighters' skill is enhanced by the use of well-equipped vehicles and advanced protective clothing.

Glass storage jars are used for fire debris samples because glass, unlike plastic, does not contain chemicals that could contaminate samples

SAMPLE COLLECTION
Collecting clues is vital to the success of any investigation. Because contaminated samples are useless for analysis in the forensic laboratory (pp. 46–47), officers carry glass jars in which to store and protect evidence.

Knob to adjust hydrogen gas flow

Reading shows how flammable the gas is

TESTING THE AIR FOR GASES
Once the fire is out, the fire investigation unit tries to find the cause. The hydrogen flame tester is used to detect the presence of flammable gases at the scene of a fire. Once it is established that a flammable gas is present, the gas can be identified and the cause of the fire determined. Within the machine, there is a naked hydrogen flame. Gas is sucked in and passes over this flame. The flame increases if the gas is flammable, and this increase is translated into a meter reading.
The degree of flammability indicates the nature of the gas.

Hydrogen gas supply

Gas is sucked into the machine through this nozzle

Gas enters small holes along this tube

Fire investigators connect this attachment to the nozzle when they are detecting gases in awkward places, such as along ceilings or floors

REASONS FOR ARSON

There are three main reasons for arson. The fire may disguise some other crime, such as robbery or murder. It may be started as an act of revenge. However, most arson attacks are associated with fraud. The number of arson fires rose during the Great Depression in the United States in the 1930s as financially troubled businesses burned their property to collect insurance payments.

Some people, like this man selling apples, did not resort to arson to raise money during the Depression

Sonic measurer

HEDGEHOG DISASTER

In Germany in 1954, Dr. Müller and his wife were driving home. Müller claimed that while he left the car to remove a hedgehog from the road, the vehicle burst into flames, killing his wife. Remains of a gasoline can found in the car and proof that Müller had been having a love affair suggested arson. Müller was found guilty of murder and sentenced to six years in prison.

IDENTIFYING THE GASES

Officers use Dräger tubes to identify gases in the air. A tube of chemicals is inserted in the pump. Air is sucked through the tube by pressing the pump. If a gas is present, the chemicals will change color. The gas is identified by comparison to a color chart.

Color change suggests gasoline fumes in the air

Pre-test tube shows the presence of a hydrocarbon – it does not identify it

Tube to identify hydrocarbons, such as paraffin or gasoline fumes

Indicates concealed, potentially dangerous, electrical wires, to be avoided when searching for clues

Metal detector

TAKING MEASUREMENTS

The accurate recording of a crime scene is essential to all investigations. This is especially important in the case of arson, where buildings may have to be quickly demolished for safety reasons. Measurements indicate the size and dimension of a location and the distance between objects. By comparing these measurements to the extent of fire damage, the officers can determine the speed and nature of the fires. A number of specialized measuring tools have been developed to give very accurate results. The sonic measurer sends sonic rays from one surface to another, measuring the distance in between.

External calipers

Vernier calipers

Magnifying glass with light

FINDING THE SOURCE OF THE FIRE

If the fire investigation unit suspects that the fire was started deliberately, a scene-of-crime officer who specializes in cases of arson is brought in. Since fires spread upward, the officer will begin at the lowest point to find the source of the fire. These officers are looking for clues near a window where an arsonist may have entered or left the building.

Meter reading indicates the quantity of flammable gas

Long rubber tube (through which the air passes) can reach into inaccessible places

In addition to operating positions, the device has Battery and Alarms settings, which enable the user to check that it is working properly

PORTABLE GAS ALARM

The portable gas alarm detects gases in the air before they are present in large enough quantities to be a fire risk. It is used in work environments that are prone to leaking toxic gases, and also by fire investigation units to ensure that the atmosphere in which they are working is safe. The hydrogen flame tester (left) is not used until it has been established that there is not enough gas in the air to cause an explosion when the naked flame is lit.

Squeezing this bulb sends the air through the alarm system

Police uniforms

Gendarme

THERE ARE TWO IMPORTANT reasons why police officers wear uniforms: first, so they can be recognized by members of the public who need assistance, and by suspects being pursued; and second, so they can identify each other and be identified by other emergency service personnel, such as firefighters, at the scene of an incident. Because climates differ throughout the world, police in different forces have different uniforms. However, all uniforms are designed to be comfortable and functional while still being formal.

U.S. police cap with sun visor for hotter climates

A sergeant wears a cloth badge with three stripes on the shoulder

U.S. POLICE
This police shirt and cap were first issued to U.S. sergeants in the 1990s. The shirt has stripes that indicate rank, a cloth badge showing the officer's department, and the officer's own metal name tag.

British "twitchers" (1610)

Come-alongs (1900s)

Police handcuffs (1990s)

Leg-irons (1902)

HANDCUFFS
"Twitchers" were used to lead the condemned from court to cell. The clever French come-along was an earlier form of the modern handcuff. Leg-irons are a variation on handcuffs. These come from a cell in an early 20th-century prison.

A British police officer's baton (1830s,

Truncheon issued in 1914 in Manchester, England

WHISTLE ALONG
Although many modern police forces rely on car and personal radios for communication, whistles are still issued, usually for traffic control. These were issued in England in the 1990s.

Thunderer whistle

Acme whistle

New York City nightstick (1990s)

British woman's baton (1990s)

British side-handled baton (1990s)

England

Australia

Ireland

Canada

Australia

New Zealand

France

United States

United States

Single star on the shoulder indicates a constable

The German Niedersachsen state police force badge,

TRUNCHEONS
Truncheons are used in apprehending criminals. The size and weight of the club depends on the situation in which it is intended to be used.

OFFICIAL BADGES
Police officers all over the world have their own badges, showing which police force they represent. These cloth badges are attached to the officers' modern-day uniforms.

GERMAN POLICE
This is the uniform of the Niedersachsen police force, one of Germany's eight state police forces. The badge on the left arm indicates which force is represented. One star on the shoulder indicates that the officer is a constable.

*Wide-brimmed
Mountie's hat*

WOMEN ON THE BEAT

This uniform is worn by a British woman police constable (WPC). The first female officers appeared on the streets in 1919, following the success of their voluntary patrols during World War I. They are now familiar sights as they patrol the streets in company with a male officer. A female officer must generally be in attendance when a female suspect is arrested, questioned, or searched.

Hard hat, suitable for riot conditions

Lanyard, or cord, that holds gun

Sam Browne (leather belt) and pouch

Handbag holds WPC's truncheon

Traditional scarlet tunic used for ceremonial occasions – working uniform is brown

Gun holster

Modern jackets and shirts are more tailored than earlier, bulky uniforms

MOUNTIES
This familiar red tunic of the Royal Canadian Mounted Police was used in 1972. In 1873, when the mounted police force was created, Mounties not only upheld the law but also acted as local counselors and mediators. Their image has slowly changed and developed and, in 1974, women joined the Mounties.

Headwear of a woman officer of the rank of assistant chief constable

Cap of the Russian militia

Silver badge of the militia

British woman's police hat

Indian police cap

British (1830s) French (1920s) Italian (1990s)

British police helmet

RUSSIAN
This cap and tunic belonged to a major in the Russian militia in 1989. The militia was responsible for policing Russia both before and after the breakup of the former Soviet Union in 1991. After 1991, Russia had to combat a huge rise in organized crime.

FROM OLD TO NEW
Although the job of the police – to keep the peace – has remained the same through time, both the uniforms and technology available for use in the fight against crime have advanced a great deal. Compare the truncheon of the 1830s with the gun of the 1990s.

Police agencies

Sheriff's badge

Hungarian warrant card

IDENTIFICATION
All officers must carry identification. It is especially important for plain-clothes officers. The identification displays the officer's credentials and photograph.

MOST PEOPLE THINK of police as either uniformed patrol officers who keep the peace on the world's streets or detectives who solve serious crimes. In fact, police forces include many specialized units formed to operate in special circumstances and conditions. Some squads, such as the Japanese riot police, the French Compagnies Republicaines de Securité (CRS), and the U.S. Special Weapons and Tactics (SWAT) units, are trained to deal with difficult violent situations. Some squads use specialized vehicles, such as helicopters, boats, motorcycles, or horses, to perform their job under unusual conditions. The overall aim is to develop a chain of interdependent units to combat crime.

ON THE BEAT
A community's safety and well-being are usually in the hands of the "beat" officers such as the French policeman here. A beat police officer patrols the streets on foot or in a vehicle, preventing crime and protecting citizens' rights to a crime-free society.

Face shield to protect against missiles

RECOVERING EVIDENCE
Many criminals seem to believe they can destroy evidence – such as a weapon – by throwing it into a canal or river. However, most police forces have trained diving units comprised of officers called frogmen. Ninety-five percent of a frogman's work is done in zero visibility, relying entirely on touch. Divers recover not only weapons but also vehicles and bodies.

Armor to protect hands in close combat

Possible murder weapon

Underwater breathing apparatus

CROWD CONTROL
In any situation where rioting crowds cannot be managed by regular police, specially trained and equipped officers are sent to the scene to restore order. In Japan, the riot police squad (above) is known for its efficiency.

HIGHWAY PATROL
High speed and maneuverability have made motorcycles an essential vehicle for the police. Most forces have trained motorcycle units, such as the Los Angeles traffic police (left), who patrol the highways and city streets.

POLICE MARKSMEN
Officers highly trained in the use of firearms work with the regular police in sieges or hostage situations. The order to shoot to kill is only given when all other options have failed, as there is always a chance of hitting a civilian. These special armed units are separate from the many officers throughout the world who routinely carry guns.

Safety helmet

MOUNTAIN RESCUE
Special police teams with climbing experience are used in some mountain areas to help with rescue work. The officers (above) work in the French Alps where they use motorcycles to travel quickly over rough ground. The motorcycles are much lighter than those used in highway patrol, similar to the trail bikes used in cross-country racing.

High-velocity rifle with telescopic sight

Officer's raincoat is kept in this leather pouch

Police horses are exposed to loud recordings of crowds and bands to get them used to noise

Riders spend half their working week grooming horses and cleaning their equipment

MOUNTED POLICE
Many countries have a mounted police branch, usually used to control crowds and to perform ceremonial duties. The first British horse patrol was a pair of mounted Bow Street Runners (p. 10) in 1763. In 1805, a larger patrol was introduced. Because of the color of their jackets, the officers were called "Robin Redbreasts." Today London's Metropolitan Police has a patrol of about 200 horses. A female rider is shown here (right).

Long baton used in riot control

CANADIAN MOUNTIES
The Royal Canadian Mounted Police was founded in 1873 as the North West Mounted Police, then renamed in 1920. The Mounties patrolled the vast prairies in the west. The intelligence and sure-footedness of the horse made it a perfect means of transport. Even today, the horse is a valuable asset.

Selected horses are three- to four-year-old hunters. Like their riders, they receive about two years' training

Detectives

THE TASKS OF INVESTIGATING a crime and identifying the culprit are carried out by detectives. Whether by interviewing witnesses or searching for the tiniest piece of forensic evidence, detectives try to reconstruct a sequence of events until they believe they know what happened. Most detectives are officers in a specialized division of the police, but many others work for private agencies. These detectives, who are often known as private investigators (PI's), can be hired by anybody to investigate anything – for a fee. The public's fascination with the detection of crime is reflected in the number of detective stories in books and on film and television. These detectives may be real or fictional characters, and their methods and equipment may differ, but they share a common pursuit: the fight against crime.

SIR ARTHUR CONAN DOYLE
Probably the world's best-known fictional detective is Sherlock Holmes, created in the 1880s by Sir Arthur Conan Doyle (1859–1930), a British writer. Holmes relied on logical deduction and attention to minute detail to solve crimes. It is less well known that Conan Doyle was also an amateur sleuth himself, and was involved in a number of major cases.

TAKING A CLOSE LOOK
Sometimes the smallest detail provides the clue that solves a crime, which is why the ability to magnify objects is so important in detection. In the laboratory, microscopes are among the most valuable pieces of equipment. Binoculars are also useful to detectives on surveillance, who must be able to see activities and people clearly without being noticed themselves.

Binoculars used by a private investigator

This knob adapts the degree of magnification to suit the user's vision

A scene-of-crime officer with a magnifying lens can identify small clues, such as hairs or cloth fibers

MAIGRET
Popular French detective Commissaire Jules Maigret of the Police Judiciaire is the main character of dozens of novels, short stories, films, and television programs. Maigret was created in 1930 by Georges Simenon, a Belgian-born writer, and has always been identifiable by his trademark pipe.

INTERNATIONAL AGENCY
Police forces around the world are centralized at Interpol (the International Criminal Police Organization), established in 1923. Police detectives can refer to computer files, fingerprints, and criminal records gathered from more than 100 member countries. Interpol's headquarters have been in Lyon, France, since 1989.

PHILIP MARLOWE
A familiar character in detective fiction is the hard-boiled, tough-talking private eye who lives a lonely life on the city's "mean streets." Philip Marlowe, created in the 1930s by Raymond Chandler, is perhaps the best-known example of the type, immortalized in novels and films.

MRS. KERNER
Annette Kerner, Britain's most famous female private detective, worked from the early 1920s to the 1950s. She became known as "the queen of disguise" and was equally convincing as a waitress in a criminals' café as she was as a socialite while thwarting a jewel theft. She once posed as a drug addict to catch a gang of opium dealers.

Allan Pinkerton

PRIVATE EYES THAT NEVER SLEEP
In 1850, U.S. detective Allan Pinkerton established the organization that has become the world's oldest privately owned detective agency – it is still going strong. The term *private eye* came from the Pinkerton trademark – the words "We Never Sleep" written under an open eye.

USING CRIME AGAINST CRIMINALS
It is not only burglars who find it useful to have a set of tools to open locks. Many detectives and undercover surveillance officers also need to get past locked doors – perhaps in the search for drugs, stolen goods, or information about a crime. The official equipment shown at left can open most kinds of locks, almost anywhere in the world.

Selection of lock-picks

File

Keyway blank

Tool for probing locks

Special telephoto lens for long-distance work

Camera's standard lens

1:4 937925

RECORDING EVIDENCE
All investigations involve the collection of a wide range of clues. Photographs are vital. They may record a meeting between the individuals under investigation, a crime in progress, or the scene of a crime that has not yet been disturbed by investigators. Most private detectives will use a telephoto lens, like the one at right, to gather evidence from a distance.

PSYCHIC DETECTION
Estelle Roberts was a famous English "psychic detective" who worked with the police. If given a victim's personal objects from the crime, Roberts could sometimes imagine the crime scene in her head, even seeing the criminal's face.

Undercover surveillance

INFORMATION IS VITAL to both the person who wants to commit a crime and the person who wants to catch the criminal. For example, the time at which a bank transfers money is as important to the bank robber as the time of a planned raid is to the law enforcement officer. In the early days of detective work, information-gathering techniques were simple. The robber, sometimes working with an accomplice inside the bank, watched and waited. The officer, with the help of informants, did the same. Today's great technological advances, however, have made the gathering of secret information easier than ever. With round-the-clock observation on closed-circuit television, telephone tapping using tiny transmitters, and advanced tracking systems that lead detectives to the thief, criminals may be seen, heard, and traced through every stage of their crimes.

THE EVER-OPEN EYE
The use of closed-circuit television (CCTV) is vital in the fight against crime. Signals are transmitted from a camera to a television screen along cables or telephone links, in a closed circuit. Cameras placed in areas such as stores and banks can provide police with accurate records of crimes being committed and lead to visual identification of the perpetrators. The introduction of CCTV in courtrooms allows some witnesses, such as young children, to be interviewed in a separate room with a live video replay in the courtroom.

WIRED FOR SOUND
This battery-operated bug (below left) is the size of a matchbox. The device, which consists of a microphone attached to a radio transmitter, is hidden. Sound signals from the bug are picked up by the radio receiver (below right), which transfers the signals to an earpiece.

Radio receiver with earpiece

A BUGGED ELECTRIC SOCKET
This electric socket looks like any other. Even with the cover removed, the miniature bugging device is not visible. The device is a transmitter that carries sound in the room, in the form of radio waves, to a distant receiving unit. Another kind of device transmits sound directly along the power cable to a receiver plugged into the same electrical circuit.

CONCEALED CAMERA
This canvas shoulder bag has been adapted to hide a video camera. One of the fasteners has been removed, leaving a hole. The camera is carefully placed inside the bag so that the lens is positioned next to the hole. The concealed camera can then secretly record images from within the bag.

Normal-size lens. Some cameras have lenses as small as match heads

Ordinary canvas sports bag

The bag is filled with clothing to protect the camera and hold it in position

Main body of bag has a hole in it, through which the camera lens receives an image

Wallet with transmitter

Magnet to cancel alarm

HIGH-TECH PURSE
If this wallet is moved, a radio transmitter triggers an alarm system. A thief trying to lift the purse from a bag or drawer would be detected immediately. A magnet passed across the wallet cancels the alarm.

This wire clips to a document and activates an alarm if the document is disturbed

Alarm

DESK TRAP
These devices alert people to thieves attempting to steal from desk drawers. The lower device has two magnets joined by a wire. One magnet is stuck to the underside of the desk, the other to the top of the drawer. If the drawer is opened, the magnetic field is broken, setting off an alarm.

Magnetic strip

Radio receiver

UV paste, which sticks well to metal

Cotton swabs for applying powders

Paintbrush for applying pastes

UV crayons for marking furniture or boxes

Gloves to protect detective's hands when applying substances

UV powder for wood or paper objects

Blue UV powder, used on blue objects

UV pen

Powders are visible when concentrated, but invisible once applied

Tweezers for holding bills or coins during application

STAKEOUT
A stakeout is an undercover surveillance operation. In this still from the film *Stakeout*, actor Richard Dreyfuss portrays a detective keeping watch. He uses binoculars, wiretaps, and other classic devices to keep crucial witnesses and suspects under surveillance.

ULTRAVIOLET DETECTOR KIT
One way to fool burglars is to mark valuable goods with a substance that is invisible under normal lighting but that shows up clearly under ultraviolet light. The thief's hands are covered with the substance after handling the goods. Another method is to use a substance that is colorless until it mixes with water. The thief touches the goods and unwittingly covers his or her hands with the substance. Gradually moisture from the hands causes a reaction and the substance becomes visible as a colored stain. Ultraviolet markers are used to write the owner's name on their possessions. If the goods are stolen and then recovered, the owner can be contacted.

Telephone tap

Tap connected to chosen line

Radio transmitter

TAPPING INTO CONVERSATIONS
It is often useful for law enforcement officials to gain access to an individual's telephone conversations. One method of tapping is to connect wires and a transmitter to the junction box outside the building. Another method is to fit a radio transmitter directly into the telephone handset, sending conversations to a receiver set.

Crime scene

THE LOCATION OF A criminal incident is called the scene of the crime. The first job of police officers at the crime scene is to seal off the area so that potential evidence is not disturbed. Once this has been done, only authorized persons are allowed within the area. The most important members of the investigation team at this point are the scene-of-crime officers (SOCOs), who use their extensive training and experience to search for clues to be sent to the forensic laboratory for examination (pp. 46–47). Forensic science is the technique of using scientific methods to solve crimes. Modern forensic science had its origin in 1910, when Edmond Locard of France formulated his "exchange principle." This theory simply states that a criminal always takes something away from the scene of the crime – or leaves something behind. The criminal may take away hair or blood from the victim, or soil (peculiar to the area) on the soles of his or her shoes. The criminal may leave fingerprints, footprints, or fibers from clothing. It is this evidence that the SOCOs collect.

MURDER!
In the case of murder, the body of the victim must be removed from the crime scene and taken for a postmortem as soon as possible. Before this can happen, the victim must be pronounced dead by a doctor. Then a forensic pathologist makes a preliminary examination. Next, a chalk or tape outline is made around the corpse so that investigators know its position. The body can then be transported to the hospital mortuary, where the autopsy takes place.

Toothed calipers enable a tight grip on wet or slippery articles

HUNTING FOR CLUES
This picture shows the hunt for information at the scene of a murder in New York. Nothing in the room has been touched or moved to allow scene-of-crime experts and photographers to record as many details of the crime as possible. A police photographer is recording relevant evidence on film, while his colleague searches for evidence that may be sent to the forensic laboratory.

THE AMPEL PROBE
This tool was designed for use by crime scene investigators. The tongs enable officers to search suspects or their property without risking personal injury (for example, from an open knife) and without damaging objects that may bear trace evidence such as fingerprints. It also is useful for removing evidence without personal contact.

Specially designed handles ensure firm grip

Evidence
labels

Shoe covers

Fingerprint
ink pad

Magnetic
fingerprint
brush
(p. 45)

Fingerprint
dusting
powder

Fingerprint
brush in
tube

SCENE-OF-CRIME KIT
As most crime scene
investigations must be
carried out at a moment's
notice, valuable time is
saved if a SOCO has a
ready-packed case of
equipment. This case
contains fingerprinting kits
(pp. 44–45) and collecting
bags and tubes to preserve
clues. A coverall, cap,
gloves, and shoe covers
are provided so that
a SOCO will not
introduce foreign
materials to the scene.

Face mask to prevent
inhalation of fingerprint
powder or harmful fumes

3M
9913
EN 149 FFP1S
CE 0086 96

Thin, sharp
edge of scalpel
can pick up
fine hairs
or fibers

Tape may be
used to
measure
breadth
of blood
splatter
(p. 42)

Angled mirror
to see behind
and under
objects

Tweezers for
collecting small
pieces of evidence

Shoe covers to prevent
investigators from introducing
foreign materials to the scene

Cap to prevent
transfer of hair

Scene-of-crime evidence-
collecting equipment

Magnifying
glass

AT THE SCENE OF THE CRIME
This officer, dressed in a plastic coverall,
protective gloves, and shoe covers, is searching
for evidence among blades of grass. He is using
tools from a scene-of-crime kit to collect
evidence. The collection of evidence can be a
laborious task at an outdoor crime scene, as there
may a very large area of ground that must be
searched for possible clues. The clues may also have
been moved or damaged by animals or the weather.

Following clues

SEEMINGLY INSIGNIFICANT traces left at the scene of a crime by the victim or criminal are vital clues that can help police in their investigations. Fingerprints, tire prints, and shoe prints can help identify a criminal; bloodstains can illustrate where or how the crime took place. Investigating officers carefully analyze every aspect of a crime scene, even clues that might not be noticed by an untrained person. More dramatic clues, such as bullet holes and broken glass, are easily noticed, but special training and equipment are needed to analyze this kind of evidence. The damage caused by weapons can also provide clues. For example, a piece of glass shattered by a bullet may leave traces on a criminal's clothes.

DROPS OF BLOOD
Marks left by blood can reveal much to the specially trained crime scene investigator. The shape of blood drops on a flat surface can indicate from what height they fell. Splashes on a wall can show the direction from which they came. Other patterns are spurts, pools, smears, and trails. These may reveal the movements of the victim and criminal, and help investigators piece together the crime.

The fired bullet is propelled along the barrel, picking up marks on its way

Marks left on the cartridge, caused by the firing pin when the gun is fired

BULLET MARKS
Cartridges consist of two parts: bullets and cases. When a gun is fired, the bullet travels along the barrel and picks up marks unique to that gun, which can be compared with a test bullet fired from the same weapon. Marks left on the base of the case by the firing pin can be compared in the same way. By comparing bullet marks, investigators can connect a particular weapon to a particular crime.

SHOE PRINTS
Shoe prints are left either as impressions in a substance such as soil, or as prints in a liquid such as blood or oil. These traces are photographed at the scene for future comparison with the shoes of a suspect. Identification points may be the patterns on the sole and distinctive signs of wear and tear.

TIRE PRINTS
Prints left by tires can be compared with the tires on a suspect's car. Like shoes, tires often have an identifiable wear pattern. Police are further helped by the fact that manufacturers use different types of tires on different models of car.

SHOTS THROUGH GLASS
Ballistics is the study of guns and ammunition. In a forensic laboratory specializing in ballistics, experts set up tests to demonstrate the effects caused by bullets fired from different distances and through different thicknesses of glass (above). Police can refer to this information when they examine a bullet hole in glass from a crime scene. It can indicate the spot from which the gun was fired.

Broken pattern in tire print suggests that two treads on the outer edge of the tire have worn down

BREAKING GLASS
When glass is smashed, the broken edges have tiny shell-shaped notches. A broken window can be fitted together like a jigsaw puzzle. A piece of glass discovered in a suspect's car can be compared to glass recovered from the crime scene. If the notches fit exactly, the glass is from the same windowpane.

REFRACTIVE INDEX
Tiny pieces of glass found on a suspect's clothing may be too small to fit into a glass jigsaw. Instead, the recovered glass can be compared to glass from the crime scene by measuring its refractive index, or the amount a ray of light bends when it passes through glass. Different kinds of glass have different refractive indexes.

Crowbar used by a burglar to force open windows or doors

DUST AND SOIL ANALYSIS
Because dust and soil are so easily carried from the crime scene – on skin, shoes, and clothing, or in the hair of a suspect – they are useful for comparison with similar substances at the scene. Both dust and soil vary greatly in their contents, often over a small area, so this analysis can prove quite accurate.

Dust   Soil

Wood chippings left at crime scene after chisel is used

Contents of vacuum cleaner bag from suspect's home may contain dust samples that match those at crime scene

Plastic bag thrown away in suspect's home may contain purchase receipt for items found at crime scene

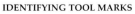

WHAT RUBBISH!
Garbage is routinely searched for evidence after a crime. For example, discarded documents, such as letters, may reveal a suspect's movements in the weeks leading up to the crime. Search of a garbage pail may result in the recovery of actual evidence, such as a weapon or stained clothing.

LOOKING AT DOCUMENTS
No two people's handwriting is the same. A handwriting expert can compare a scribbled note to a handwriting sample from a suspect. A seemingly blank page may contain indents from writing on the previous page, which has been torn off. This, too, can be used to identify a suspect.

Chisel, used to force open a lock

IN THE LABORATORY
Forensic laboratories usually specialize in one particular branch of science, such as biology, chemistry, or ballistics. Some of the equipment is specific to that subject, but most laboratories rely heavily on comparison microscopes (pp. 46–47). This busy laboratory (left), like most other labs, has evidence from hundreds of crimes awaiting analysis.

IDENTIFYING TOOL MARKS
Marks are sometimes left by an implement, or tool, used to force open a door or window at a crime scene. Because the tool is harder than the wooden frame, it leaves an impressed imprint of its shape. Sometimes this can be matched to a tool owned by a suspect – particularly if it has a distinctive shape or marks of previous damage.

Fingerprints and DNA

MANY EARLY CIVILIZATIONS were aware of the unique nature of the ridges and furrows on the tips of the fingers. Chinese potters, for example, signed their work with a fingerprint. However, it was not until 1858 that William Herschel, an English civil servant in India, claimed that no two person's fingerprints are the same, and that they do not change with age. During the late 19th century, researchers developed a method of classifying prints so that they could be easily identified. Just as fingerprints are unique to an individual's fingertips, so deoxyribonucleic acid (DNA) is unique to every cell of an individual's body. In 1984, scientists began to create DNA profiles, sometimes called genetic fingerprints, from body fluids, flesh, skin, or hair roots. By matching the genetic information from a forensic sample with that of a suspect, investigators can prove a suspect guilty or innocent.

FRANCIS GALTON
Sir Francis Galton (1822–1911) was an English scientist who made the first advances in identifying the basic patterns of fingerprints. Sophisticated modern methods are based on the classification system he devised during the 19th century.

Roller to transfer ink to plate

Fingerprint ink

INK AND ROLL
The universal method of taking a suspect's fingerprints is called ink and roll. A thin coating of black ink is rolled onto a metal plate. Then, one by one, each of the subject's fingertips is rolled on the ink from one side of the nail to the other, then rolled onto a white chart, producing prints.

Lifting tape to remove prints from surface

Aluminum dusting powder, which reflects light and photographs well

BRUSHING UP
If fingerprints have been left in a substance such as blood or paint, they are easy to see. However, most prints are made by the oils and sweat on the surface of the skin and are almost invisible. The most common technique for revealing these fingerprints is to dust a fine powder over the surface, which sticks to the oily deposit. The powder-covered prints are removed from the surface on transparent sticky tape and then photographed. This officer is dusting for prints on a stolen car.

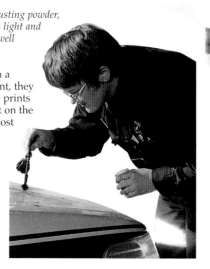

Fan-shaped brush for larger areas

Brush used with very fine powders

Long-handled brush for reaching into corners

Delicate "whisper" brush used with aluminum powder

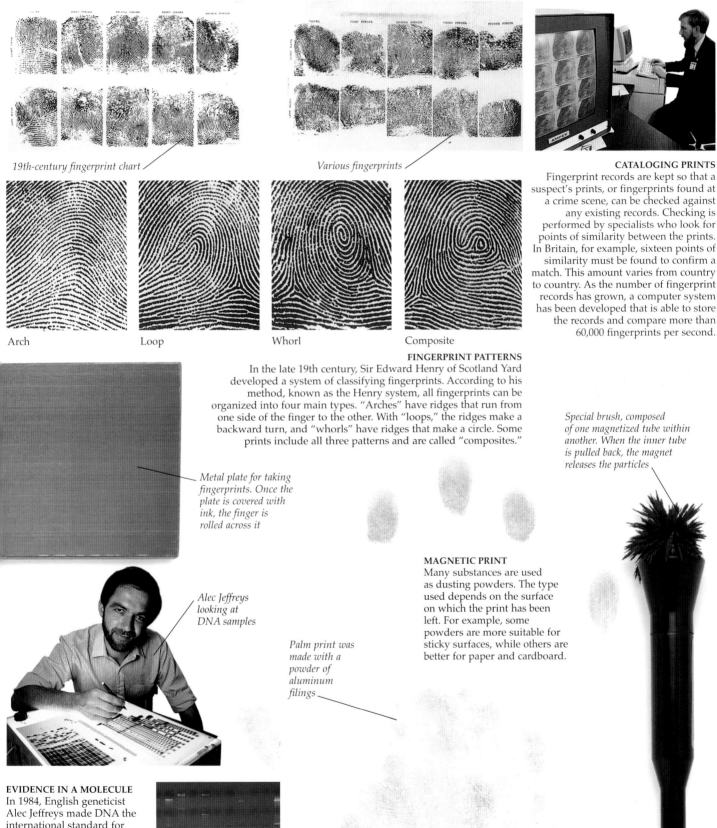

19th-century fingerprint chart

Various fingerprints

CATALOGING PRINTS
Fingerprint records are kept so that a
suspect's prints, or fingerprints found at
a crime scene, can be checked against
any existing records. Checking is
performed by specialists who look for
points of similarity between the prints.
In Britain, for example, sixteen points of
similarity must be found to confirm a
match. This amount varies from country
to country. As the number of fingerprint
records has grown, a computer system
has been developed that is able to store
the records and compare more than
60,000 fingerprints per second.

Arch

Loop

Whorl

Composite

FINGERPRINT PATTERNS
In the late 19th century, Sir Edward Henry of Scotland Yard
developed a system of classifying fingerprints. According to his
method, known as the Henry system, all fingerprints can be
organized into four main types. "Arches" have ridges that run from
one side of the finger to the other. With "loops," the ridges make a
backward turn, and "whorls" have ridges that make a circle. Some
prints include all three patterns and are called "composites."

*Special brush, composed
of one magnetized tube within
another. When the inner tube
is pulled back, the magnet
releases the particles*

*Metal plate for taking
fingerprints. Once the
plate is covered with
ink, the finger is
rolled across it*

MAGNETIC PRINT
Many substances are used
as dusting powders. The type
used depends on the surface
on which the print has been
left. For example, some
powders are more suitable for
sticky surfaces, while others are
better for paper and cardboard.

*Alec Jeffreys
looking at
DNA samples*

*Palm print was
made with a
powder of
aluminum
filings*

EVIDENCE IN A MOLECULE
In 1984, English geneticist
Alec Jeffreys made DNA the
international standard for
identification. He discovered
that within a single DNA
molecule there is a sequence
of information unique to each
individual (except identical
twins, who have the same
DNA). Like fingerprinting,
DNA profiling can be used
to connect a suspect with
the scene of a crime.

BIOLOGICAL "PATTERN"
From a sample of any human tissue
or body fluid, a biological "pattern"
of that person can be created. This
is called a DNA sample and looks
like a supermarket bar code.

Forensic analysis

DESPITE DEVELOPMENTS IN technology, the basic principles of forensic science have remained the same. A forensic scientist's main task is comparison. For example, the scientist will compare a hair found at a crime scene with one from a suspect's head, or match a fabric fiber found in a suspect's car with the clothing worn by a victim. The main techniques used are microscopic examination and chemical analysis. A forensic laboratory will use several types of microscopes in their work; electron microscopes can magnify objects more than 150,000 times, which makes identification and comparison easier. Comparison microscopes are used, allowing a scientist to view two samples side by side through the eyepieces. Other types of microscope can help compare bullets to determine their source, or identify minerals and drugs. Forensic laboratory work combines many different disciplines, such as biology, chemistry, ballistics (the study of guns and ammunition), and document analysis.

NAPOLEON'S DEATH
Napoleon Bonaparte's death in 1821 was ascribed to stomach cancer. However, there have been persistent rumors that he was poisoned. In 1960, a forensic team analyzed a lock of Napoleon's hair taken from his head when he died. More than 13 times the normal level of arsenic was found. The poison could have been administered deliberately, or ingested by accident.

Laser lamp used to detect the presence of proteins, found in body fluids

SEARCHING FOR SALIVA
Forensic scientists often look for evidence left at murder scenes. The pillow (above) has been sprayed with a substance that binds with protein. The protein will fluoresce under the laser lamp, showing the presence of body fluids, such as saliva. The pillow can then be sent to the laboratory for DNA analysis (pp. 44–45).

Human eyebrow magnified 500 times

Green cotton fibers and yellow polyester fibers magnified 1,000 times

Dog hairs magnified 1,000 times

Extracting solvent absorbs poisons as urine sample is spun

IN THE LABORATORY
The forensic laboratory is one of the most valuable tools in a crime investigation. Clothing, shoe prints (pp. 40–41), dust traces, weapons, and bullets are a few items that may be analyzed in the crime laboratory. This scientist is using a comparison microscope. Originally designed for the comparison of bullets and cartridge cases, it is now used to compare almost any kind of evidence. Two slides carrying samples are placed on the viewing tray. The slides are viewed simultaneously through the eyepieces.

Scientist examines some fibers in an evidence bag under the microscope

Centrifuge spins at a rate of 2,000 to 3,000 revolutions per minute

Left-hand column is a control. It is included as a guideline to help identify substances in the sample extracts

The control is made up of a mixture of three pure drugs. The middle one is methadone

IDENTIFYING POISONS

Thin-layer chromatography is a technique used to identify the various components in poison and drug samples extracted from body fluids. A glass slide is coated with silica gel, and spots of the sample are applied just above the bottom edge. The slide is lowered into a tank containing a liquid that reaches just below the line of sample spots. As the liquid rises up the gel (just as water rises through blotting paper), it carries with it the different components of the sample. As different substances rise at different rates, each sample is separated into a series of dots rising up the slide. Each dot is a different component of the sample. The slide can be compared with previous results and the components identified.

This spot shows there was nicotine in this sample

Shirt may smell of gasoline suggesting a possible cause of the fire

Chromatogram of five sample extracts

This column is a sample from a drug abuser's urine. The highest spot is methadone

The arsonist's hair may be found on the shirt

SHIRT SLEEVE

This burned shirt sleeve, taken from the victim of a suspicious fire, will be sent to the laboratory. The autopsy had already proved the victim died before the fire started – there was no soot in the lungs, so he had not breathed smoke. Scientists will test the fabric to determine if it had an accelerant, such as gasoline, on it. Such a finding would strengthen the theory that the fire was started deliberately in an attempt to hide a murder.

SEPARATING SAMPLES

High-speed microcentrifuges are used to separate postmortem samples into their component parts. For example, an extracting solvent is added to a sample of blood in a test tube. The tube spins at high speed in the centrifuge. The solvent extracts any foreign substance, such as poison, from the blood. The lighter component (the poison absorbed in the solvent) rises to the top of the tube, while the heavier component (blood) sinks to the bottom. The solvent can then be tested to identify the poison.

Sample of stomach contents

Sample of urine

Sample of blood

BODY FLUID SAMPLES

If the postmortem examination of a body suggests poisoning, the pathologist sends samples of bodily fluids and parts of the vital organs to the laboratory for analysis. Tests will reveal whether the body contains poison, what the poison is, and how much of it is present.

MT97—56301

MT97—55233

The bare bones

FEW PEOPLE REALIZE HOW MUCH information an expert can glean from a pile of bones – information that can help solve a crime. Examination of a skeleton can reveal the gender of the deceased, as male and female skeletons have different skulls and pelvic (hip) bones. Even without a complete skeleton, height can be calculated within an inch (25 mm) by measuring the long bones (the femur in the leg or the tibia in the arm). Age can sometimes be determined from the way in which sections of the skull have closed together, or, up to the age of 25, from the development of the teeth. The structure of the head, face, teeth, and long bones can also indicate the indigenous group of the deceased.

MIKHAIL GERASIMOV
Mikhail Gerasimov was a pioneer of facial reconstruction in Russia during the 1950s. The reconstruction of Tamerlane the Great, the Mongol king, was Gerasimov's greatest achievement. In the illustration above, Gerasimov (left) and an archaeologist examine a 30,000-year-old skeleton.

Cast of the skull, made of alginate

Work starts with the temples and the neck

Building the nose is very demanding

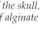

Wooden pegs

1 The skeleton of a young woman was dug up in Wales in 1989 and named "Little Miss Nobody" by the police. To begin the facial reconstruction, a cast of the skull is made. Then pegs are inserted at fixed points to indicate the standard thickness of the flesh.

A male sacrum is narrower than a female sacrum

2 Plastic balls make "eyes" and the "flesh" is built up in clay. With the shape of the skull and the length of the pegs as guides, the muscles of the face begin to form.

3 After the mouth, the areas around the eye sockets are carefully filled in. Then the nose is formed. Because there are few bones that indicate the shape of the nose, this is one of the most difficult parts of the reconstruction.

4 The clay has now been filled out to the tops of the guide pegs and the sculptor is ready to put the finishing touches on the head. All that remains is to smoothe the surface to give a more lifelike appearance. If the age of the person at death is known, the sculptor can texture the skin correctly. The whole process takes little more than a day to complete.

HIS AND HERS
Men and women have different skeletons. Male skulls have a little lump at the back of the head called the nuchal crest and another on the forehead called the suborbital ridge. The sciatic notch on the hips is wider on the female skeleton than on the male. The sacrum, at the bottom of the spine, is smaller in males than females.

LASER RECONSTRUCTION
The use of laser technology in the re-creation of faces was pioneered by forensic pathologist Dr. Peter Vanezis, seen here demonstrating a new system in London, England. When Karen Price was identified, Dr. Vanezis used a laser technique to superimpose a photograph on the skull made by Richard Neave. They fitted perfectly.

THE FACE MAKER
Richard Neave is a medical illustrator from Manchester University in England. Although Neave's early work was with archaeological remains – he rebuilt the head of King Midas – he has recently worked with the police on building the faces of murder and accident victims. Neave is seen here working on the skull of Karen Price.

Even if the hair length is known, it is impossible to tell the style

Although just a guess, Karen's hairstyle proved quite accurate

5 Photographs of the facial reconstruction were published in police notices and newspapers, and broadcast on television. As a result, a name was put to the anonymous skeleton. She was identified as Karen Price by a Cardiff social worker. Later, two men were charged with Karen's murder.

Experience and instinct enable the sculptor to reconstruct the soft tissues of the nose, lips, and ears

The sinews of the neck can be determined from the bone structure

DENTAL IDENTIFICATION
Because teeth are almost indestructible, they can often be used to identify a body when other methods cannot (for example, following a fire or an air crash). A panoramic photograph, like this one, is taken of the surviving teeth and matched to the victim's dental record. As no two people have identical dental histories, this method is accurate.

Attention to detail

THERE ARE FEW "OPEN AND SHUT" cases – crimes where it is known immediately what happened, who did it, and why. Investigators usually put together a case from lots of small clues. Often no detail is too insignificant. A witness may remember the color or make of a car, or even its license plate number. An onlooker may have noticed something about a suspect – his or her voice, a physical feature, or a distinctive tattoo. Sometimes a witness recalls the criminal's distinctive clothing or jewelry. These eyewitness details are added to the other clues picked up by scene-of-crime officers and forensic scientists and built into a case to be presented later in court.

LINEUP
Lineups are used by police throughout most of the world. A suspect takes any position in a line of other people of similar appearance. The witness is then asked to identify the suspect. Lineups are not always reliable. If the real criminal is not there, a witness may choose the person who looks most like the criminal.

This "bar print" represents the sound made by a person saying the word baby

DISTINGUISHING MARKS
Members of gangs often like to have some way of identifying fellow members. Tattoos are a good means of identification because they cannot easily be erased. Tattoos are used by members of Chinese secret societies, such as the Triads. Individually chosen tattoos are even more useful to the police, because no two people are likely to carry the same pattern of markings.

Death's head (skull) rings are popular with motorcycle gangs

VOICE RECOGNITION
Each human voice has a unique "print." The current system of recording and identifying voiceprints was developed during World War II. In the bar print above, the horizontal axis records the length of time, the vertical axis measures the strength of the sound. Voiceprints can be used to identify a suspect in cases of abusive telephone calls or demands for ransom payments made by phone.

Photographic strips of eyes

Photographic strips of noses

A 19th-century mug shot

"MUG SHOT" BOOK
After photography's invention in the mid-19th century, one of its most important uses was to allow police to keep visual as well as written records of criminals. This is one of the earliest examples of a mug shot book, from the City of London Police. At that time, similar records were being kept in the United States, under the direction of Thomas Byrnes of the New York Police. In France, Alphonse Bertillon (pp. 52–53) was improving the French system by photographing criminals.

COMPUTER-AIDED VIDEO-FIT
Improved computer technology has led to the videofit, which replaces Photo-fit identification. Above, a witness is selecting the general hairstyle of the suspect. This choice is transferred to the video screen, where it can be altered to give a closer likeness. Another recent development makes the video-fit three-dimensional so that it can be seen and altered at different angles.

LICENSE PLATES
All countries have a system of matching vehicles to their owners. This information can be used by the police to check whether a vehicle has been stolen or reported at a crime scene, and to find out about the owner. Many criminals put false plates on cars to avoid detection. The British plate above is false. The numbers are too small and thick, making them difficult to read. The middle plate is a temporary French plate. The letters *WW* show it was issued to a person moving to a new home.

False British plate

Temporary French plate

German export plate

These numbers indicate that the vehicle should have left the country by September 1996

Billions of different faces can be made by combining various strips

One strip that will make the nose of a Photo-fit

SELECTING EACH FEATURE
This selection of just two pairs of eyes, two noses, and two mouths from a Penry Photo-fit kit shows how much features can differ. The kits have about 100 different eyes, noses, and mouths. This collection represents only a small proportion of the huge variety that exists in people's features. Unlike the video-fit, Photo-fit just gives the "feeling" or "look" of a person, rather than a close representation.

A photographic strip of someone's hairline

The Photo-fit

The original subject

PHOTO-FIT CASE
In 1971, Britain introduced the Penry Facial Identification Technique (Photo-fit). British forensic scientist Jacques Penry's kit consisted of photographic strips of different eyes, noses, mouths, jaw lines, hairlines, and ears. These features were put together by the crime witness and a police expert. The resulting Photo-fit was circulated, often leading to a conviction.

MAKING UP A FACE
To demonstrate the Photo-fit method, a "witness" was shown an ordinary member of the public (above right) and then asked to construct the portrait (above left) from memory. In a real crime situation, a traumatized witness may not remember the exact appearance of a criminal. For this reason, eyewitness identification has become devalued.

Criminal characteristics

FOR HUNDREDS OF YEARS scientists have investigated the theory that certain people are born to be criminals. In the mid-19th century, anthropology, the study of humankind, became a popular science. Anthropologists studying the field of abnormal behavior examined various types of criminals to see if they shared any physical characteristics. One of the early researchers was a French prison doctor named Lauvergne, who made plaster casts of his patients' heads to demonstrate their "evil" features. Most of Lauvergne's work was found to be incorrect. However, at the same time, Alphonse Bertillon, working for the Paris police force, was also taking detailed measurements of criminals' heads and bodies, but for a different purpose. He was using the measurements to identify known criminals, rather than to create a physical profile of a criminal type.

"SHERLOCK HOLMES OF THE COUCH"
Dr. James Brussel, an American criminal psychiatrist, has been called "the Sherlock Holmes of the couch." Brussel was a pioneer in psychiatric profiling – a method of deducing a criminal's characteristics by studying the way a crime is carried out. Dr. Brussel used his theory successfully to help solve many crimes. He helped capture New York's "Mad Bomber" in 1957 (below) and helped catch Albert DeSalvo, the "Boston Strangler," in 1963.

WITCH HUNTS
In medieval times, it was thought that all witches had certain characteristics, such as warts or moles. Women thought to be witches were subjected to the ducking chair – being immersed in water while tied into a chair. If they did not drown, it was thought to prove they were witches, and they were executed anyway.

According to Gall, the brain is divided into seven main sections, each with a specific purpose (for example, intellectual or domestic)

Within each brain section, there are several areas that represent different functions, such as friendship and courage

THE MAD BOMBER
In 1940, George Metesky began a 16-year series of bombings to seek revenge on his previous employer, who he believed had wronged him. The accurate description of Metesky given by Dr. James Brussel led to Metesky's arrest (above). Metesky was found unfit to stand trial and was committed to a state hospital for the criminally insane.

PHRENOLOGY
In 1796, Dr. Franz Gall, a doctor in Vienna, announced his theory of phrenology, in which a person's qualities and abilities are traced to particular areas of the brain. Gall believed that while people thought, their brains and skulls changed shape, causing bumps on the surface. Phrenologists thought a person's character could be understood by studying the shape of the skull. This pseudoscience was initially popular, but was soon rejected as false.

CESARE LOMBROSO
An Italian psychiatrist of the mid-19th century, Cesare Lombroso made a study of 7,000 criminals in order to prove that different "criminal types" could be identified by physical characteristics. For example, he believed that swindlers and bandits had larger-than-normal heads, and that thieves and highwaymen had thick hair and beards. He never proved his theories despite the elaborate instruments he invented in order to do so.

ALPHONSE BERTILLON

Bertillon was an assistant clerk in the records office of the Judicial Identification Service in the Paris police force when, in 1883, he proposed his theory of anthropometry ("man measurement"). Bertillon concluded that no two human beings have exactly the same measurements, and he devised a method of identifying criminals by comparing records of individual physical attributes. Bertillonage was adopted as a general system in France. However, it was soon replaced by fingerprinting (pp. 44–45).

Double-headed calipers for smaller measurements

MEASURING GAUGES

Bertillon's father was a doctor and had a room full of scientific instruments for measuring the body. The younger Bertillon found these instruments fascinating. When he began to experiment for himself, he collected his own set of calipers and gauges, which he later used to test his theory of anthropometry. These gauges, right, and calipers, left, are the types Bertillon used.

NOSES CHARACTERIZED BY THE EXTRAORDINARINESS OF ONE OF THEIR DIMENSIONS

Original Bertillon "mug shot" book

BOOK OF FEATURES

Another of Alphonse Bertillon's successes was recognizing the value of the newly invented science of photography. Prior to this, the visual appearance of criminals was recorded in words, called a *portrait parlé*, or spoken picture. It became possible to assemble classified books of photographic portraits. Looking at these, witnesses could identify criminals These are the predecessors of mug-shot books, commonly used today.

Gauge for larger measurements

Measurements of suspects are taken in the Bertillonage room of the police headquarters

Photographs of the criminal from the front and side

CRIMINAL RECORD

Bertillon's clerks kept detailed files that included names, addresses, and crimes committed. Also recorded were various measurements of parts of the body. Eventually, photographs of the criminal, including both front and side views, were attached. This method of presenting full-face and profile shots is now used throughout the world.

BERTILLONAGE AT WORK

Within three months of proving his theory of anthropometry, Bertillon used his method to convict a thief named Dupont. Dupont had been brought to the police station, on a charge of theft. Bertillon measured him and recognized the results. Dupont had been convicted of theft before and measured by Bertillon. However, during the first arrest, Dupont was using a different false name. Bertillon's method proved it was the same person, and this was enough to convict him a second time.

An elaborate kind of a ruler for measuring smaller parts of the body, such as fingers

Following a scent

DOGS HAVE A SUPERIOR SENSE OF SMELL to humans, and their keen noses have made them useful colleagues in the police fight against crime. By following an individual's unique and invisible scent, dogs are able to track down his or her whereabouts. Police forces train dogs to chase, grab, and hold a suspect, and then release the suspect on command. Dogs have been used to track criminals for a long time. References to police dogs can be found in the 19th-century writings of Charles Dickens and Sir Arthur Conan Doyle, and in the 19th-century United States, dogs were often used to hunt escaped convicts and runaway slaves. During the 20th century, the role of the canine detective has grown. Police and other law enforcement agencies now train dogs to sniff out drugs and explosives.

BLOODHOUNDS
Traditionally, tracking human beings has been the bloodhound's special skill. Commissioner Sir Charles Warren introduced bloodhounds to London's Metropolitan Police in the 1880s. To test the bloodhounds' ability, Sir Charles acted as quarry to see if the dogs could track him down. They did – and one of them bit him! However, bloodhounds have now been replaced by lighter, more agile breeds.

CHECKING A CAR
Many vehicles travel around the world on ships and ferries. At ports, specially trained sniffer dogs inspect vehicles for illegal substances such as drugs. Here, a dog is checking the engine compartment of a car.

SUSPICIOUS SUITCASE
Airports also face smuggling problems. Dogs are used to search baggage holds. They are trained to recognize and detect the scents of contraband items such as drugs or bomb-making equipment. The dog alerts its handler if it picks up a suspicious scent.

SUPER SENSE
All around the world customs and excise authorities (pp. 28–29) use dogs to sniff out illicit chemicals. Springer and cocker spaniels and Labrador retrievers are commonly used to hunt out substances such as cocaine and marijuana. However, sniffer dogs hunt not only for drugs. The U.S. Department of Agriculture has its own "Beagle Brigade" to search for illicit fruit and meat in airports.

Springer spaniel wears reflector harness when working in restricted light

Most popular police dog breed is the German shepherd

SPECIAL TRAINING
Only puppies with good temperaments are selected for the rigorous training that a police dog must complete. A 14-week-old puppy is given to a handler, who takes it home to become part of his or her family. When the dog is one year old, it receives 14 weeks of basic training, during which it is taught to obey voice and hand signals and to track and hold a fugitive. The training also involves fitness exercises to build the dog's stamina and agility.

REX III
Perhaps the best-known of all police dogs was Rex III, whose exploits in England during the 1950s are almost legendary. Rex III made more than 130 "arrests" and was the first dog to work with the famous Flying Squad and to be trained to detect drugs. During his active service, Rex III was awarded many honors and medals.

FINDING A VICTIM
During the blitz of London in World War II, sniffer dogs were used to locate people buried beneath the debris of bombed buildings. Dogs are also used in murder investigations to locate the victims' bodies.

Camera and lights

Harness is specially designed to be comfortable and lightweight

ON THE TRAIL OF A SUSPECT
Like police horses (pp. 34–35), dogs are trained to ignore loud noises such as gunfire. During their training, police dogs are taught the best way to attack and to avoid being clubbed by a weapon. Sadly, many brave animals are still killed in the line of duty.

Battery pack to power lights and camera

LIGHTS, CAMERA, ACTION
Besides their superior sense of smell, sniffer dogs have another advantage over humans – they can search very small spaces. This dog is going to search a small area on the other side of a trapdoor. The animal is fitted with a special harness that contains a small video camera, lights, and a battery pack. This allows the handler to see the interior area.

Instructor wears protective padding

ARRESTED BY A DOG
Police dogs are taught to attack a suspect only on the command of their handler. During their training, police dogs learn how to restrain a suspect by the arm. An instructor, wearing heavily padded sleeves to prevent injury, plays the part of the fleeing suspect. Despite their efficiency when attacking, police dogs have gentle natures.

Dog practises attacking many times during training

Outlaws

It is a strange fact that some of the worst criminals in history have become popular folk heroes. One of the best examples is Dick Turpin (p. 14), a murderous thug who terrorized travelers in the countryside around London during the 18th century. He became a romantic figure after the publication of *Rookwood* (1834), a novel written by Henry Ainsworth in which Turpin was portrayed as a chivalrous highwayman riding his trusty horse, Black Bess. Books are not the only inspiration for hero worship. Some people long for the freedom of an outlaw, and admire his or her daring. More recent antiheroes range from the Great Train Robbers (p. 17) to India's Bandit Queen (below).

ROBIN HOOD
England's most legendary outlaw, Robin Hood, robbed the rich and gave to the poor. There is no evidence that he actually existed; the stories of Robin's adventures are based on medieval ballads that have been embellished through the centuries. He has remained popular and has become the subject of numerous films, such as *The Adventures of Robin Hood* (above), 1938, starring Errol Flynn as the notorious outlaw.

LOUIS MANDRIN
Louis Mandrin was one of the best-loved smugglers France has ever known. In the 1740s, he formed a gang of 2,000 men, who were so well trained that they often defeated the king's troops. Mandrin's dashing adventures made him the people's hero. He was captured in 1755 and was executed by being tied to a large wheel. His limbs were crushed as the wheel turned, and he was left to die.

BUTCH AND SUNDANCE
Butch Cassidy and the Sundance Kid were members of the outlaw gang the Wild Bunch, who operated during the 1890s in the western United States. From their hideout, the Hole in the Wall, they specialized in large-scale horse and cattle rustling and armed robberies of banks and trains. These outlaw gangs were always popular with the public, but Butch and Sundance became particularly well known after a romanticized film was made in 1969 (right).

In the 1969 film Butch Cassidy and the Sundance Kid, *Butch was played by actor Paul Newman*

The Sundance Kid was played by actor Robert Redford

A film has been made, called Bandit Queen, *about Phoolan Devi*

THE BANDIT QUEEN
Phoolan Devi, also known as the Bandit Queen, was imprisoned in 1983 in India for banditry and murder. A rebel against her fate as a low-caste woman, Devi became a heroine to thousands of Indians. Once released, she fought politically for women's rights.

Butch Cassidy's real name was Robert LeRoy Parker

Sundance's real name was Harry Longbaugh

Bonnie Parker's body armor, found on the ground near the car in which she and Clyde were shot

The back of Bonnie Parker's body armor

Bonnie and Clyde had removed their body armor while they ate lunch

A bullet hole made during the final shoot-out

Body armor made of bullet-proof material

Floyd Hamilton's rifle

BEFORE THEY MET
Clyde Barrow was born into a poor Texas family in 1909. He was already under arrest for robbery when he met Bonnie Parker. She came from a more respectable family, had married and been left when, at the age of 19, she met Clyde. In 1932, the pair began their dramatic but short-lived partnership.

Clyde's watch

Miniature boots made by Clyde Barrow for his mother

Photographs of Blanche Barrow

Blanche wrote of her advancing blindess in later years on the back of this photograph

BONNIE AND CLYDE
In 1932, Clyde Barrow and Bonnie Parker teamed up to become the most infamous pair of robbers and murderers of the decade. They terrorized the southwestern United States, murdering at least 13 people. In 1934, Bonnie and Clyde were ambushed by police officers, who killed them by firing 150 gunshots into their car.

GANG MEMBERS
Clyde's brother Buck and sister-in-law Blanche were also members of the gang along with robber Floyd Hamilton. Buck was shot dead in 1933, while Blanche was captured and imprisoned. In 1938, Hamilton was sentenced to 20 years in Alcatraz (pp. 12–13).

A WANTED poster put out for Bonnie and Clyde

Strange but true

LINDOW WOMAN
In 1983, a badly decomposed female head was dug up at Lindow Moss in Cheshire, England. Frightened by the discovery, a local man confessed to the police that he had killed his wife 23 years before and buried her in the peat bog. In fact, when the remains were scientifically dated, they were found to be more than 1,770 years old.

CRIME AND THE LAW are serious subjects. However, crime also has its share of lighter moments and strange stories. Sometimes criminals are just foolish – such as armed robber José Sanchez. In 1995, when police arrived at the scene of an armed robbery in New Jersey, they found a piece of paper that the robber had used to wedge open the door of the building. It turned out to be a traffic ticket issued to Sanchez the night before the robbery, and it had his name and home address printed on it. There are other crimes that are strange because of the daring or ingenuity of the criminals, or because of the motives that inspired them. For example, in 1981 John Hinckley attempted to assassinate President Ronald Reagan in an effort to impress actress Jodie Foster, with whom Hinckley was obsessed.

ON BOTH SIDES OF THE LAW
Welshman Henry Morgan was a famous buccaneer in the Caribbean of the 17th century. With the unofficial support of the English government, he spent over 10 years attacking Dutch and Spanish colonies in the area. In 1670, Morgan raided Spanish-owned Panama. Because the raid took place after a peace treaty between England and Spain, he was arrested, transported to London, and charged with piracy. Relations with Spain soured, and King Charles II pardoned and knighted Morgan, then sent him back to Jamaica as deputy governor.

AVENGING "NAILS" MORTON'S DEATH
Dion O'Banion (above) was one of Chicago's most notorious gangsters, and Samuel "Nails" Morton was his most loyal gunman. Morton had been awarded the Croix de Guerre during active service in World War I and was considered indestructible. However, Morton was thrown by a horse and killed while riding in Lincoln Park. In revenge, O'Banion sent gunmen to kill the horse.

Tilh was tried, found guilty, and hanged

Jodie Foster and Richard Gere starred in the 1993 film Sommersby, *which was loosely based on the story of Martin Guerre*

FAKE IDENTITY
After having disappeared for eight years, Martin Guerre returned in 1556 to his home in the French village of Artigat. He was welcomed by all except his uncle, who insisted that this Martin was an impostor. Guerre's uncle was right. Arnaud du Tilh had met Guerre, got a detailed picture of his life, and adopted his identity. Tilh almost got away with it – until the real Martin Guerre came back.

MURDERING THE PRESIDENT
In 1963, President John F. Kennedy was assassinated in Dallas, Texas. Lee Harvey Oswald was arrested for the crime. However, because it was not a federal crime to murder the president, neither the FBI nor the Secret Service could take Oswald into custody. Instead, he was taken to a Dallas county jail, where, because of lapses in security, he was shot dead before he could be put on trial.

DK EYEWITNESS BOOKS

1–110

Future updates and editions will be available online at www.dk.com

EYEWITNESS BOOKS

A–Z

SCIENCE

ASTRONOMY

CHEMISTRY

EARTH

ECOLOGY

ELECTRICITY

ELECTRONICS

ENERGY

EVOLUTION

FORCE & MOTION

HUMAN BODY

LIFE

LIGHT

MATTER

MEDICINE

SKELETON

TECHNOLOGY

TIME & SPACE

SPORT

BASEBALL

FOOTBALL

OLYMPICS

SOCCER

SPORTS

ANIMALS

AMPHIBIAN

BIRD

BUTTERFLY & MOTH

CAT

DOG

EAGLE &
BIRDS OF PREY

ELEPHANT

FISH

GORILLA,
MONKEY & APE

HORSE

INSECT

MAMMAL

REPTILE

SHARK

WHALE

HABITATS

ARCTIC & ANTARCTIC

DESERT

JUNGLE

OCEAN

POND & RIVER

SEASHORE

THE EARTH

CRYSTAL & GEM

FOSSIL

HURRICANE &
TORNADO

PLANT

ROCKS & MINERALS

SHELL

TREE

VOLCANO &
EARTHQUAKE

WEATHER

THE WORLD AROUND US

BUILDING

CRIME & DETECTION

FARM

FLAG

MEDIA &
COMMUNICATIONS

MONEY

RELIGION

SPY

Future updates and editions will be available online at www.dk.com

DK EYEWITNESS BOOKS

SUBJECTS

HISTORY

AFRICA

ANCIENT CHINA

ARMS & ARMOR

BATTLE

CASTLE

COWBOY

EXPLORER

KNIGHT

MEDIEVAL LIFE

MYTHOLOGY

NORTH AMERICAN INDIAN

PIRATE

PRESIDENTS

RUSSIA

SHIPWRECK

TITANIC

VIKING

WITCHES & MAGIC-MAKERS

ANCIENT WORLDS

ANCIENT EGYPT

ANCIENT GREECE

ANCIENT ROME

AZTEC, INCA & MAYA

BIBLE LANDS

MUMMY

PYRAMID

THE BEGINNINGS OF LIFE

ARCHEOLOGY

DINOSAUR

EARLY HUMANS

PREHISTORIC LIFE

THE ARTS

BOOK

COSTUME

DANCE

FILM

MUSIC

TECHNOLOGY

BOAT

CAR

FLYING MACHINE

FUTURE

INVENTION

SPACE EXPLORATION

TRAIN

PAINTING

GOYA

IMPRESSIONISM

LEONARDO & HIS TIMES

MANET

MONET

PERSPECTIVE

RENAISSANCE

VAN GOGH

WATERCOLOR

Acknowledgments

Dorling Kindersley would like to thank:
David Roberts; Ross Simms and the Winchcombe Folk and Police Museum; Sam Tree of Keygrove Marketing Ltd.; Assistant Divisional Officer Derek Thorpe and the Fire Investigation Unit at Acton Police Station; Rentokil Pest Control; Dr. Brian Widdop of the Medical Toxicology Unit Laboratory; Shona Lowe of HM Customs and Excise; The Metropolitan Police Museum; Mike Wombwell; the Commissioner for the City of London Police for his kind permission to photograph Penry's Photo-fit Kit; Bill Harriman of JWF Harriman.

Researcher: Robert Graham

Design and editorial coordinators: Vicky Wharton, Jayne Parsons, Miranda Smith

Design and editorial assistance: Goldberry Broad, Darren Troughton, Jake Williamson, Julie Ferris, Nancy Jones, Susila Baybars

Additional photography: Geoff Dann, Gary Ombler; Richard Shellabear

Photographic assistance: Gary Ombler, Andy Kamorovski

Index: Marion Dent

Jacket: Mark Haygarth

Picture Credits
The publisher would like to thank the following for their kind permission to reproduce their photographs:

(a = above, b = below, c = center, l = left, r = right, t = top)

Action Plus: Glyn Kirk 18cl.
Archive Photos: 19ca, 24tr; Lambert 19r.
Archive Photos France: 21ca, 35tr.
J.S.G. Boggs: 59tl.
The British Council: Anita Corbin & John O'Grady 45clb.
The British Film Institute: © Warner Bros. 56tr.
The British Museum: 14tr, 20tr, 20cb, 20crb, 21cr.
Bruce Coleman Collection: Luiz Claudio Marigo 28br.
Camera Press: Lionel Cherruault 50cl; Dennis Stone 29tl.
Christies Images: 22bc.
Corbis: Bettmann 14bl, 14br, 37tr; Bettmann/UPI 24bl, 24br, 25tl, 25br, 52tr, 52cr; Everett 36bl.
Courtesy of Diners Club International: 19c.
E.T. Archive: British Museum 12tr; Tate Gallery 20br.
Mary Evans Picture Library: 8tl, 10br, 11cl, 12tl, 13tl, 14cr, 14bc, 16bl, 19cb, 22tr, 22cl, 24cl, 28cl, 28bl, 29br, 36tl, 44tc, 45tl, 46tl, 52bl, 52br, 53crb; Explorer 9tl.
Fortean Picture Library: Dr. Elmar R. Gruber 9tr.
The Ronald Grant Archive: © United Artists 37tl; © Warner Bros. 58bc.
Robert Harding Picture Library: 34bl; FPG International 31tl.
David Hoffman: 29tc, 31cr, 45tr.
Hulton Getty: 8cl, 8cra, 8bl, 11tl, 16tl, 16cr, 17tl, 17tr, 18tr, 23tl, 23tc, 23tr, 23cl, 23cra, 33br, 53tl, 56cl.
The Image Bank: Barros & Barros 40tr.
The Kobal Collection: © Touchstone Pictures 39cra; © 20th Century Fox 50tr, 56br.
H. Keith Melton: 37c.
Metropolitan Police Service: 34br, 35c, 54cl, 55tl.
Microscopix: Andrew Syred 46cll, 46cl, 46c.
Moviestore Collection: © United Artists 15cl.
News International Associated Services: 21br, 23crb.
Rex Features: 42crb, 54bl, 59c; Hugh Routledge & Peter Bennett 51tl; Nils Jorgensen 43bc; Julian Makey 55cra, 55br; James Morgan 55c; John Shelley 35bl; Sipa/Dieter Ludwig 56bl; The Times 35tl; Today 46bc, 47cr.
Science Photo Library: 49br; American Science and Engineering 29tr; Klaus Guldbrandsen 45bl; Peter Menzel 40clb, 46tr; Hank Morgan 50cr.
Service de l'Information et des Relations Publiques: Tanguy Delamotte 34tr.
Frank Spooner Pictures: 59tr; Gamma/G. Bassignac 41br; Georges Merillon 54 clb; Olivier Pighetti 15tl, 15tr; Olympia/Palazzotto 27tl.
Sygma: Rufo 27cr; Sion Touhig 55tr.
Telegraph Colour Library: 30tl; Ron Chapple 44bl; Colorific/Tim Graham 33brr, 34cl.
Topham Picturepoint: 12bl, 12cr, 37tc, 37bl, 48tr, 58bl, 58cl, 58cr; Associated Press 25bl, 26bl, 26br, 27tr, 26tr; Press Association 49tl.
Roger-Viollet: 8br, 36br.
Jerry Young: 48cll, 48cl, 48cr, 48br, 49tr, 49c, 49cr.

Jacket: Hulton Getty, inside front bc.

Index

J.S.G. Boggs's drawing of an English five-pound note

ESCAPE FROM THE COURTROOM
On the night of July 17, 1976, Albert Spaggiari robbed the bank Société Générale in Nice, France, after breaking in through the underground sewer system. Spaggiari was captured and put on trial for his crime, but he made a dramatic leap from the dock and slipped out through a window. During his 12 years on the run, Spaggiari hid behind homemade disguises like the one above.

FORGER OR ARTIST
In October 1986, J.S.G. Boggs, an American artist, was showing his work at London's Young Unknowns Gallery. To everyone's surprise, the police arrived and seized the pieces, which were drawings of English bank notes. The Bank of England prosecuted under the Forgery and Counterfeiting Act, but Boggs was acquitted.

BUTTERFLY LAW
Most countries have rules about killing certain species of wildlife. In California, there is a law intended to protect butterflies. City Ordinance Number 352 in Pacific Grove makes it a misdemeanor to "kill or threaten a butterfly," such as the swallowtail above.

J.S.G. Boggs holding some of his drawings of bank notes

Italian, U.S., and English currency

INTERNET SWEET-SHOP
A 15-year-old boy from Dublin, Ireland, used his parents' computer to order candy from a U.S. company via the Internet. When the company asked for a credit card number, the boy simply made one up. Unfortunately, it was the real account number of someone in Argentina, and $2,000 worth of chocolate arrived at the boy's home. Since the culprit was a juvenile, he was not charged.

"TITANIC" THOMPSON
In April 1912, when the liner *Titanic* struck an iceberg off Newfoundland, 1,513 lives were lost. One who did not perish was Alvon Clarence Thompson. Since women and children had priority in the escape, Thompson dressed as a woman to make sure of a place in a lifeboat. After his return to the United States, Thompson began to collect on the insurance policies of the *Titanic*'s victims, whom he claimed as relatives.